Gareth Shute is a music journalist who has published four books on music and the arts through Penguin/Random House, as well as writing regularly for Lonely Planet. He is also a musician and has toured internationally as a member of indie groups, the Ruby Suns and the Brunettes.

CONCEPT ALBUMS

Gareth Shute

IP
Investigations Publishing

ACKNOWLEDGEMENTS:

Thanks to my wife, Mieko Edwards, and proof-readers, Simon Comber and Mike Stachurski, as well as cover designer, Baly Gaudin and to Rex McGregor for his helpful advice. Thanks also to photographers Gary Brandon and Bruce Jarvis. I am also grateful to Aubrey Powell at Hipgnosis and Peter Curzon at Storm Studios.

Copyright © 2015 Gareth Shute
Published by Investigations Publishing
First published 2013

All rights reserved. No part of this publication may be reproduced, stored in any retrieval system or transmitted in any form or by any means, electronic, mechanical, photocopying, recording or otherwise, without the prior permission of the copyright owners.

Cataloguing-in-Publication Data
Concept Albums / Gareth Shute
174 p. ; 18 cm
ISBN – 9781517287559
1. Popular-history and criticism. 2. Rock music-history and criticism.
781.66-d23
Cover design: Baly Gaudin

CONTENTS

Introduction 7

Chapter One – The Birth of the Concept Album 22

Chapter Two – The Arrival of Prog 54

Chapter Three – Concepts of the Future, Concepts of the Past 81

Chapter Four – Pink Floyd & the Legacy of Prog 104

Chapter Five – The Metal Years 135

Chapter Six – Hip Hop & Alternative Rock 163

Chapter Seven - Concept Albums in the New Millennium 185

Introduction

The idea of a 'concept album' first emerged in late sixties to describe records which tied together all their tracks under a single over-riding narrative. Yet the first difficulty in starting this book is that there was never a clear definition given of what this phrase actually referred to. Like so many labels in popular music criticism, the tag was created by music journalists so they could bunch together a handful of disparate albums and thereby attempt to capture the current zeitgeist of the moment.

The term was applied loosely and so it's hard to undertake a clear discussion of the subject without reconsidering what was going on at the time when the idea of concept albums first came up. It's worth putting ourselves back into the headspace of the time and trying to conceive what music journalists at the time were really trying to capture by using this term. At the same time, we need to recognise that the term has had a remarkable staying power and is still used to refer to many modern releases.

The reason why concept albums were held up as being important initially was that they were a clear representation of the fact that popular musicians were beginning to delve into more complicated musical works – using extended themes and storylines in a way that was more associated with classical music or stageshow musicals. Psychedelic innovators were attempting to harness the unabashed energy of popular music, while simultaneously pushing beyond the three minute pop song to take up complex compositional structures and unusual lyrical approaches. The standard pop music subject – love won and lost – was cast inside and musicians drew instead from tripped out imaginings, spiritual visions, and dreams of a better future. The album itself became the art-form, rather than any particular song.

Yet, it was often the case that these musicians had little knowledge of how to carry out a musical statement on a large scale and so their work was put together from imaginative fragments rather than a coherent structure, tending towards the outlandish over the humdrum, relying on creative leaps rather than having any clear plot in mind. If a storyline became stuck then there was always the option of having something fantastical take place out-of-the-blue so that the plot is able to progress.

The early creators of concept albums seldom followed the creative writing mantra to 'write what you know' unless this involved singing about endless nights of snorting, injecting, smoking, and drinking, as well as the inevitable fallout of all this hard living. Nonetheless, if their central idea was fresh enough and was supported by a dazzling musical backdrop,

INTRODUCTION

then they were able to produce an album that was able to expand in the listener's mind to create a whole new landscape of sound and imagery.

When most people think about concept albums, they picture prog aficionados playing overblown thirty-minute epics or late-period hippies singing about tripped-out, psychedelic journeys. Yet, recently the form has been embraced by musicians from a wide range of genres, including punk act Green Day, indie darlings Arcade Fire, hip hop diva Janelle Monáe, and distraught theatrical rockers My Chemical Romance. These artists have helped spawn a renaissance of the concept album, which seems to be part of a general attempt to keep the traditional album format relevant in an age when digital technology has made it just as easy for consumers to purchase only the individual tracks they enjoy most.

The arrival of iTunes in 2003 had many music commentators speculating that it would cause the 'death of the album' and within four years, the New York Times reported that digital sales had overtaken CD sales for the first time, while in the downloads market, singles sales were outstripping albums sales at a rate of 19 to 1.

Despite this trend, many musicians were still not willing to simply move from single to single. This tension was captured by Simon Frith (chair of judges for the UK's prestigious Mercury Prize) when he told the Guardian: 'There's an interesting divergence between musicians' continuing commitment to album making and audience's apparent reluctance to buy albums. It's partly cost and, even more, convenience. People listen in a way that is more mobile and more distracted, and therefore single tracks make sense.'

This led some artists to react to this situation by stitching their albums together with a central theme, which provides a way to ensure that each song contributes a crucial element to the larger work. Just when the album seems ready to be buried, concept albums are making a comeback.

Defining a 'concept album'

So what exactly does the phrase 'concept album' refer to? The general understanding of the term is that it refers to an album with songs that cohere around a single idea. This form of fuzzy description allows almost any album to be called a 'concept album' since artists usually have some central ideas that they are currently interested in when they go into the recording studio to create a new work. Albums have always worked best when their songs feed off each other and the concept album takes this to its logical extreme by introducing an overarching theme that ties each track together, though a clearer line of demarcation is needed if we are going to discuss the subject with any clarity.

I'm sure there'll be plenty of readers who think my definition of a concept album is too restrictive, but without drawing some clear outlines, the subject can soon explode and we soon end up including a huge amount of works that don't have any similarity to the ones that inspired the phrase in the first place.

Pop music goes conceptual

One starting point might be that the term 'concept album' eventuated from popular music, since it was first used by music journalists to refer to works from the psychedelic era, though it has since been applied across the fields of folk, country, metal, and hip hop. This fact is important since it shows that concept albums have a separate history to musicals and light operas, even if they are sometimes cast in a similar light (leading to the term 'rock opera').

The key difference is that musicals are written to be performed on the theatrical stage, while concept albums are created to be stand-alone musical works (even if they are sometimes turned into musicals, just as musicals are sometimes released as albums). What's more, musicals are usually fronted by a cast of singers each playing a different role and backed by an anonymous ensemble of musicians, while a concept album is usually the sole creation of a band and is performed as such. The development of both forms grew independently of one another, though some cross-pollination certainly occurred.

The emergence of musicals can be traced back to the 1880s, when operettas and musical drama split off from opera to create a new form. Musicals eventually began to incorporate jazz music, but it took until the late 1960s for a fully-fledged rock

CONCEPT ALBUMS

opera (*Hair*) to be produced, so the adoption of rock music in musicals actually took place around the same time as concept albums were first emerging from within rock.

When rock'n'roll first made an impact on popular music in the fifties, it wasn't considered to be a serious form of music and so the idea of this genre being used to create immense musical epics would've seemed quite preposterous. Most musicians had very little control over their own work and relied on recording compositions by other songwriters, which meant they were unable to purposefully write a complete set of tracks around one theme.

It would be another decade before the idea of a concept album was able to emerge, though if we apply the term retrospectively then we can see that a few artists – such as Woody Guthrie, Lee Hazelwood, and Johnny Cash - were already beginning to use themes to group songs together as an album. The reason they were able to apply this level of control was because they were working as self-reliant songwriters and were hence free from the limitation of going from single-to-single.

The scope for early concept albums was very limited in Guthrie's day, since there was no possibility to carry the theme across to the album artwork. Up until the late 1940s, record packaging was simply a plain slip (a dust cover) with a circular section removed in the centre so the label of the record was visible. If there were images on this slip then it was usually

INTRODUCTION

Johnny Cash was making 'concept albums' before the phrase was coined. *(Bruce Jarvis)*

advertising for the record label rather than anything provided by the artist and only classical music or jazz were seen as being worthy of being packaged in illustrated sleeves. The term 'album' came about due to the fact that long classical works were often spread across multiple records, held together in a set of sleeves like an album of photos (though these seldom had an actual book of pages, so the term 'album' was a misnomer from the start).

In contrast, early rock'n'roll was driven by the lightweight 7-inch, 45rpm single. Only once an artist had a few successful singles could they look at putting these together on a long-player (LP). This restricted rock and pop musicians to working song-by-song. However, the rise of pin-up singers gradually altered the way album covers were treated, since record labels found they could sell more copies if they printed a photograph of pop artists on the sleeve of their records.

The social changes of the sixties gradually opened up more opportunities and musicians realised that they could do a lot more within the album format. A single track could span the whole of a side, like an orchestral piece or long jazz composition. Rather than just using a stock photograph of the artist/band, they began to manipulate these images or replace them entirely with art-works (following in the footsteps of many jazz and classical records).

This progression of cover art is exemplified by The Beatles: *Help* (1964) shows a realistic shot of the band; *Rubber Soul* (1965) uses a warped photo of the band with bubbly text style for the

INTRODUCTION

title; *Revolver* (1966) is a surreal black-and-white drawing of the group that has been integrated with a number of smaller photographs. The following year they used the album packaging to even greater effect by coming up with a way to tie the cover image to songs that the album held. For *Sgt Pepper's Lonely Heart Club Band* (1967), Paul McCartney wrote a song introducing the fictional band of the title and then suggested that he and his bandmates dress up in colourful regimental regalia to impersonate the group for the cover shot, surrounded by cut-out images of other famous or respected figures.

The completed album was only vaguely conceptual, but it laid a blueprint for the artists that followed. It showed the potential for concept albums to create a mythology around an artists' work, taking them beyond a simple set of songs to become an interconnected unity, in which each element of the music, lyrics, and artwork add more depth to the listener's experience.

In 1968, the sales of albums surpassed those of singles and musicians took advantage of their audience's broadening attention span. One notable example was The Who and their hugely influential work, *Tommy* (1969). Lead songwriter, Pete Townshend developed a firm plot across the individual songs and the album sleeve provided a written expurgation of the storyline.

Yet, many subsequent concept albums were not so clearly constructed and used central themes rather than firm plots to hold them together. One example of this type of 'themed' concept album is *Tales From Topographic Oceans* (1972) by Yes, which was loosely inspired by an Indian religious text and was given a coherent form through its use of repeated melodic structures. It went on to become one of the most successful double-albums of all time, despite its inscrutable subject matter and complex musical arrangement – in fact, its notoriety is one of the reasons that progressive ('prog') rock is so often associated with concept albums. It is therefore helpful to distinguish those that have a 'narrative' or storyline and those that are tied together more loosely around a theme.

Narrative versus thematic concept albums

If we look back to the early concept albums by Woody Guthrie (about the dustbowl refugees from Oklahoma) and Lee Hazlewood (about a fictional town called 'Trouble') then we find that they are essentially held together by a theme rather than a narrative (even if there are storytelling elements within individual songs). This is probably why they don't spring to mind as influential concept albums, since it was the bold narrative works of the psychedelic era that pushed the form into the popular consciousness. It was only with the arrival of prog that the term was loosened to include albums that were tied together in a more abstract way.

Narrative and thematic concept albums do have one thing in common - they both introduce non-musical ideas to structure an album. This is important because it isn't really meaningful to call something a concept album if its tracks are only linked by musical approach or style or a compilation of pre-written songs that happen to share a similar subject matter.

To understand this point, we again need to think back to the birth of the phrase 'concept album' in the late sixties. The records which spurred this term in the first place were ones that were purposefully written to cohere around a single idea. Music journalists were trying to capture a sudden leap in the aims of popular songwriting – rather than just working song-by-song, musicians were taking a single idea and using it to inspire every single track on an album.

What a concept album is not

To express more clearly how the intent of a songwriter to create a thematic or narrative work is essential to whether we call something a 'concept album' or not, it is worth looking at some albums that have been labelled under this title, but which do not really fit as neatly as you might think at first.

The first type of misuse of the label is when it just refers to a set of songs that are only grouped by their genre – as when the soul singer Ray Charles recorded a country album. The style of music may have been unusual for him, but it was genre that tied the tracks together rather than a concept from outside of music.

This is also true of albums that collect together cover versions of songs by other composers around a single theme. Frank

Sinatra is often cited in lists of artists who've released concept albums because he released many themed albums early on – most notably *In The Wee Small Hours* (1955) which focuses on a late night sense of loneliness or *Come Fly With Me* (1958) which is a musical trip around the world. Yet none of his albums were purposefully written as a cohesive work. The songs were in fact composed by a variety of songwriters and collected together retrospectively, so the *intention* to write a conceptual work simply wasn't there. If we included this album as a concept album, then we would have to let in a raft of compilation albums that have been thrown together around a theme (e.g., collections of songs about driving such the 1990 compilation, *Cadillac'n'Roll,* or every Christmas compilation ever put together).

It also needs to be made clear that if a work is only held together by the unintentional influence of what a songwriter has been going through in their own life then this is not enough to make it conceptual. Listeners might discern that Beck's *Sea Change* (1998) is about a relationship break-up, but it is clearly not a concept album (despite what Wikipedia might tell you) and this goes equally for Bob Dylan's *Blood on the Tracks* (1975). What is important that there is clear intent to write a thematic work, rather than this just being a result of the artist's circumstance at the time of writing. In fact, love songs are so prevalent that they can almost be considered as a genre unto themselves, with break-up tracks existing as a sub-genre among them. Many musicians channel their relationship crises into their music, but calling each of these a concept album would soon become meaningless.

Nonetheless, even within some of the most fantastical narrative albums, it is possible to detect elements from the writer's autobiography. One of the most well-known concept albums, *The Wall* (1980), draws directly from the life of the main songwriter, Roger Waters, but it weaves these elements together into a strong fictional narrative. The desire to draw from autobiography can also be seen in the wide range of albums that tell the story of a rock star struggling with their newly found fame and the heavy drug use that sometimes goes along with this lifestyle. This is especially common within heavy metal, where examples include – Alice Cooper's *From the Inside* (1978), Savatage's *Streets: A Rock Opera* (1991), and W.A.S.P.'s *The Crimson Idol* (1992). In each of these cases, the songwriters go behind just letting autobiographical details seep into their work and manage to construct thematic works that deserve being considered as complete concept albums.

It isn't surprising that artists often fall back on their own experiences to create their storylines, since maintaining a solid focus over an entire album is a difficult endeavour. The singular focus required often means that these works are driven by one central songwriter and this can cause problems if they are working within a band context. There is less room for collaboration and this can mean that the creator of the piece begins to alienate his bandmates. This certainly happened during the recording of the Genesis album, *The Lamb Lies Down*

On Broadway (1974). Peter Gabriel struggled to convince his bandmates to go along with his ideas: 'Once the story idea had been accepted we had all these heavy arguments about the lyrics. My argument was that there aren't many novels which are written by committee. I wrote indirectly about lots of my emotional experiences in *The Lamb* so I didn't want other people colouring it.'

This tension between one songwriter's singular vision and the desire of their bandmates to be involved is why creating a concept album has often brought groups to the brink of breaking up, or seen the songwriter themselves parting ways with the group that they had previously led, as happened to both Peter Gabriel and Roger Waters.

It should come as no surprise that musicians who've spent their lives writing short rock tracks, often have little idea about how to unfold a narrative over a whole collection. This results in plot lines that are often wildly inventive, but clunky in their construction. Yet, the music can give the stories an emotional resonance that is able to smooth over any jarring plot elements. The best concept albums inspire the listener's own imagination to fill in any gaps in logic and hence draw a greater meaning from the sometimes tenuous connections between songs.

Given the difficulty of the task, we might ask why so many musicians have attempted concept albums. For some early practitioners, it was a way to continue the musical experimentation of the sixties by taking on a new creative challenge. Other musicians were simply drawn to the bombast

INTRODUCTION

and showiness of connecting their music to a fantastical storyline – for David Bowie it allowed him the chance to recreate himself as a fictional character, while for ELP, Parliament, and Pink Floyd it provided an excuse to introduce massive stage props. This extravagance also explains why the form fell out of favour when punk and (later) grunge brought back a raw, back-to-basics approach to rock music.

Yet, concept albums were not killed off during the eighties and nineties, but were instead kept alive by heavy metal artists who weren't so shy of being outrageous. It was as if the concept album went underground, only to re-emerge in the new millennium, eventually spreading across a wide range of genres, from hip hop to electronica to metal to alternative rock.

The predicted death of the album gave artists even more impetus to return to the form as a way of showing the power of albums to make larger creative statements.

The ongoing interest in concept albums can also be attributed to their ability to push the listening experience beyond what an ordinary line-up of songs can provide, since the listener is encouraged to trace out every ounce of meaning from the music, lyrics and artwork to piece together the world that the musicians have created in embryo. Often these factors result in a sense of mythology growing up around a group, which goes beyond their role as musicians and this is why the most successful concept albums continue to draw in new listeners, providing a long-lasting legacy for the artists that recorded them.

Chapter One

The Birth of the Concept Album

The concept album is a creative form that requires the songwriter to have a large amount of control over the music they are creating and how it is packaged. In the early years of popular music, musicians were at the whim of record companies and managers so this level of control was difficult to achieve.

One early exception to this was Woody Guthrie, who lived like a troubadour – playing shows to provide himself with an income, rather than trying to fit into the wider music industry. His compositions often took their structure from traditional folk songs, but altered the lyrics to fit with contemporary situations. His album, *Dust Bowl Ballads* (1940), focuses on the movement of farmers (nick-named 'Okies') from Oklahoma to California following the dust storms of the 1930s. Guthrie himself had been part of this migration and at the time that he recorded it in New Jersey, he was known within the nearby New York live scene as the 'Oklahoma cowboy.' His songs approached the consequences of the mass migration from a wide range of angles – describing how it was a cause of the crime spree of

Pretty Boy Floyd and singing about the character, 'Tom Joad, from Steinbeck's dust bowl novel, *Grapes of Wrath*.

Other artists of this era had less opportunity to create themed works because they relied on performing tracks that were written by specialised songwriters and hence weren't able to invest the lyrics with any overall theme. Jazz artists often released albums that were organised around a certain theme, but these were usually collections of cover versions rather than purposefully written song cycles.

In other cases, artists released instrumental work that purported to be inspired by a single subject, but which was only dimly related to the actual sound of their work. Examples might include: Duke Ellington's *Black, Brown, and Beige* (1943), which was inspired by the history of African American people; and the early albums by surf guitar group, The Ventures, which ranged from collections of outer space themed tracks to another that covered the colours of the rainbow. One might also mention Joe Meek's attempt to envisage what living on the moon might sound like on his debut album, *I hear a new world* (1960). The tracks do include some vocals, though they are sped up to sound alien (one of many aspects that make this work sound retro rather than futuristic when you listen to it now).

Meanwhile, the example laid down by Woody Guthrie helped inspire country singer, Johnny Cash, who was also interested in American history and the roots of its folk music tradition. Cash combined these interests by recording themed albums throughout the early sixties, using a mix of his own compositions and folk standards that fitted along with these. While it might be argued that the use of cover versions means that these works can't truly be called concept albums, it seems justified in this instance since Cash wrote at least half of the tracks on each of the albums mentioned below and often used spoken intros to tie each successive song back to the main theme.

This series began with *Ride This Train* (1960), which described how the expansion of the train network had helped tame the Wild West. He then looked at the years of hard labour (some of it conducted by prison labour gangs) that was involved in forging America as a new nation on *Blood, Sweat And Tears* (1963). However, his most affecting album of this period was *Bitter Tears (Ballads of the American Indian)* (1964) which was a set of songs about the struggles of the Native Americans. Many of the songs were written by Cash's friend and fellow country singer, Peter La Farge, including 'The Ballad of Ira Hayes' about the Pima Indian soldier who helped raise the flag on Iwo Jima but later died as a poverty-stricken alcoholic. When radio stations ignored the single, Cash took out an ad in Billboard magazine asking them: 'Where are your guts?' The resulting press coverage gave a boost to the single, which finally managed to break into the Billboard Top Forty. The power of Cash's concept albums gradually faded as time went on and there was only the vaguest connection between the gunslinger tales on his album *Johnny Cash Sings The Ballads Of The True West* (1965) or the travelogues on *From Sea To Shining Sea* (1968).

THE BIRTH OF THE CONCEPT ALBUM

Mining from a similar vein was Lee Hazelwood, who'd initially made his name as a record producer for artists such as Nancy Sinatra and Duane Eddy. His first solo release was *Trouble Is a Lonesome Town* (1963), which described a small country town called 'Trouble' in the Wild West of America. Hazelwood provided a spoken word introduction for each track, describing the character that it was based upon.

While country music may have had a tradition of storytelling works, this did not exist within the newly emerged genre of rock'n'roll. During the first half of the decade most rock bands stayed close to their roots in Rhythm and Blues, with its emphasis on punchy, three-minute tracks. As the sixties progressed, the opportunities for musicians expanded and they began to take inspiration from the mood of creative freedom that had been introduced by the growing counter-cultural movement. Unfortunately the music industry wasn't setup to support experimentation. Bands were expected to write and record their songs quickly, so they could keep studio costs down and ensure they weren't kept too long away from touring (which provided a major source of their income).

Against this backdrop, it is easier to see why the Beatles were the first rock band to attempt a concept album. They had decided to quit touring because their shows had become more of a spectacle than a performance and the screaming of their female fans often drowned out the meagre output of the stadium speakers of the time. Instead they promoted their music through filming short live clips (often mimed) which could be played on television. This left them with more time to spend in the studio and their immense popularity meant that their record company was willing to allow them the largesse to follow their inspiration where it led them. The result was *Sgt Pepper's Lonely Hearts Club Band* (1967), which would plant the seed for the concept albums that followed.

Paul McCartney had written the title song after visiting the West Coast of the US and finding that all the new hippie bands had started taking peculiar, unwieldy names (e.g., The Chocolate Watchband, Big Brother and the Holding Company, Lothar and the Hand People). He wrote a song that introduced Sgt Pepper's band and arranged for a reprise of this number to bring the theme back at the end of the album. He also suggested that they dress up as the fictional band for the cover photo, while the album itself was made to sound more like a live show by having a sample of applause between the opening title track and the one which followed ('A Little Help From My Friends').

John Lennon later admitted in an interview with Playboy magazine that the album didn't really deserve to be called a concept album: '*Sgt Pepper* is called the first concept album but it doesn't go anywhere. All my contributions to the album have absolutely nothing to do with this idea of Sergeant Pepper and his band, but it works because we said it worked, and that's how the album appeared. But it was not as put-together as it sounds, except for Sergeant Pepper introducing Billy Shears and the so-called reprise. Every other song could have been on any other album.'

Sgt Pepper's proved that just the hint of a central concept could be enough to spark the imagination of listeners and create a sense of cohesion across an album. In the late seventies, the core of *Sgt Pepper's* was turned into a film, which tried to create a more solid plotline around the songs. It was a high-profile endeavour that starred the Bee Gees and Peter Frampton, with Steve Martin, Aerosmith, and Alice Cooper in supporting roles. Unfortunately, the script was poorly conceived and the acting was abysmal, causing the film to fade quickly from the public memory.

Sgt Pepper's wasn't the Beatles' only contribution to the concept album. They also showed the way forward with the medley of songs on the second side of *Abbey Road* (1969), which used repeated melodies to bind the different tracks together into a larger work. The expansiveness of these musical experiments was well suited to the contemporary zeitgeist. The year, 1967, was the 'Summer of Love' and kicked off a period in which musicians were focused on creating work that introduced new sounds and ideas into the popular consciousness. In the UK, the concept album came to be seen as one way that popular music could push into new ground and create a more mind-expanding, 'trippy' listening experience.

The Psychedelic era

One major change during the psychedelic era was that record companies began to find that youth culture was running ahead

The Beatles' hysterical fans meant they quit touring and put their energies into their studio work, which led to the faux concept album, *Sergeant Pepper's Lonely Hearts Club Band.* (Alexander Turnbull Library)

THE BIRTH OF THE CONCEPT ALBUM

of them and the only way they could remain hip was to allow musicians more freedom to keep up with the steadily changing mood of the times. The Moody Blues were emboldened by this cultural shift and explicitly disregarded their record company's wishes when they came to record their breakthrough work, *Days of Future Passed* (1967).

The Moody blues were signed to Decca, who proposed the group should record a version of Dvořák's 'New World Symphony' with the London Festival Orchestra. The release was planned as a marketing tool for the label's new stereoscopic sound recording technique and the label assumed the band would go along with this plan since it had been three years since their breakthrough hit, 'Go Now', and they were rapidly heading towards obscurity.

Despite this, the band convinced their assigned producer that their own songs would provide better material for the project. They had recently written a track called 'Dawn is a Feeling' which used the arrival of a new day as a metaphor for the start of a new relationship. The band decided to carry this idea across the album by writing about the progression of a single day, though the overall impression was more symbolic than narrative. The sense of unity across the album was supported by the dramatic interlinking sections that the orchestra played to connect one track to the next, using the song melodies as starting points and modulating between the different keys of each subsequent song.

Their record label weren't initially impressed with the finished product and put the album out as a budget price LP. Only their US label representative saw the potential of the group's sound, which he thought would perfectly fit with the new medium of FM radio that was taking hold in the US. He was proved correct when the album's finale piece, 'Nights In White Satin', went on high-rotate throughout the country, capturing the attention of listeners with its stirring multi-layered vocals and dramatic atmosphere. The orchestra didn't play on this track, though it still retained a lush sound through the use of mellotron – a state-of-the-art instrument that looped sections of tape reel, each relating to a different note, which were then were triggered by the corresponding note on a piano keyboard.

The success of *Days of Future Passed* allowed the Moody Blues to shed the image that they were just leftovers of the British Invasion and instead they were reborn as the new guard of the psychedelic era. It would be their only cohesive concept album, though other works were theme-driven - the strongest example being *To Our Children's Children's Children* (1969), which incorporated images of space-travel and reflected on the future of the human race.

A month before *Days of Future Passed* hit stores, an even more complete concept album was released, *The Story of Simon Simopath* (1967), by Nirvana, which was the first truly-realised narrative concept album. Needless to say, this 'Nirvana' is not the same outfit that made its name in the early nineties and, in actual fact, this group's music was at the opposite end of the spectrum from their grunge namesakes – they used acoustic instruments to create a form of psychedelic folk music, which was upbeat and playful.

The Story of Simon Simopath was broadly representative of the storytelling approach taken by most psychedelic artists – it started in a realist mode, but soon began introducing fantastical imagery and out-of-the-blue plot twists. Psychedelic music was supposedly inspired by drug-induced visions and there was a growing interest in mysticism, mythology, and the occult, but this imagery was difficult to contain within a coherent plot line. Instead, musicians introduced outlandish twists to keep the stories moving forward and, rather than supplying a satisfactory conclusion, they relied on surrealistic endings to bring them to a close.

In the case of *The Story of Simon Simopath*, the storyline was whimsical and imaginative, but its overall plot quickly abandoned any forward momentum and instead spiralled away into obscurity. Simon Simopath is a young boy who dreams of being able to fly but, by the second track, the storyline has skipped forward to show him as a grown man in the midst of a mental breakdown. He is hospitalised, but escapes by taking a rocket ship into the sky, where he befriends a centaur and falls in love with a tiny goddess named Magdalena.

Nirvana's music fitted the quirky theme, using chirpy, folk melodies that were carried by swirls of cello, viola, and French horn. Unfortunately the odd lyrics made it difficult for any of the singles off the album to gain traction and Simon's tale was too convoluted to capture the attention of the wider public. The band were successful enough to release a few more albums before disbanding, though they re-emerged in the 90s, partially supported by the money they'd gained from an out-of-court settlement with the newly emerged Nirvana.

Many of the elements of *The Story of Simon Simopath* are also present on *S.F. Sorrow* (1968) by The Pretty Things – in both cases, the title also refers to the main character of the piece and the plotline follows his descent into madness, though S.F. remains grounded in reality for a longer period. Like Nirvana, The Pretty Things draw from folk music, though even when they're playing acoustic numbers, the band retain a crackling edginess that made them one of the heavier bands of the British Invasion. The lyrics don't attempt a full account of the storyline and instead outline major events in S.F.'s life, which is outlined in a more detail on the record sleeve. The tale begins with S.F. being born into a working class family at the turn of the 1900s. As soon as he comes of age, he joins his father working at the 'Misery factory' and is only able to survive the gloominess of this job by focusing on his growing romance with a cute girl who lives across the road from him. Their relationship is cut short when he is enlisted in the army to fight overseas, though they eventually plan to meet up in America ('Amerik'). She takes an airship across the Atlantic but it explodes en route and S.F. falls into a deep depression. Unlike Simon Simopath, his ensuing decline into madness doesn't give him any relief and

THE BIRTH OF THE CONCEPT ALBUM

the visions he receives from a voodoo priest just confirm that society has no use for an old man like him. S.F. is left as the 'Loneliest Man in the World.'

The recording sessions for *S.F. Sorrow* had taken place at Abbey Road studios while the Beatles were still at the other end of the building finishing *Sgt Pepper's* (and another of the rooms was concurrently being used by Pink Floyd; see Chapter Five). Meanwhile, at Olympic Studios on the other side of the city, The Small Faces, were also attempting a story-based album that was intended to show that their gritty, stomping tracks could be harnessed to a larger purpose. All the songs on *Ogden's Nut Gone Flake* (1968) were originally intended to make up one complete piece, but writing the songs dragged out for a year-and-a-half before the band downgraded the project to a single side of the album. The first song of this side introduces us to 'Happiness Stan' who is disturbed to find that half of the Moon has disappeared, so he goes to find out what has happened to it. When he stops for a sandwich, a fly lands nearby and suggests that he should seek the wisdom of an old hermit. The final song outlines the hermit's philosophy, which is along the lines of 'don't worry, be happy.'

Given its limited nature as a concept album, *Ogden's Nut* would hardly be worth mentioning at all, if it wasn't for a number of innovative factors that the band introduced. Firstly, the album had a narrator – the comedian, Stanley Unwin - which added to the sense of this being a fairytale for stoners. Unwin also took part when the band performed the full cycle of songs for French television show, *Colour Me Pop* (though the music itself was mimed). One of the most revolutionary aspects of the album was its innovative cover art, which showed an ethereal set of images taken from the quest of Happiness Stan. Despite holding a single record, it's cover folded out like one for a double-album (making it a 'gatefold' cover) and it was modelled directly on the art-work of the 'Ogdens' Nut-brown Flake' tin which the band members used to keep their marijuana in. Early pressings of the album even had a circular cover (to make them the same shape of the tobacco tins), though this infuriated record store staff, who found that they would easily roll off their shelves. The gatefold design had previously been used for a number of other psychedelic albums (including *Sgt Pepper's*), but never had it been used so strikingly (it would go on to be a standard format within prog rock).

The albums up to this point had each pushed the form forward, but for the notion of the concept album to really capture the wider public's imagination, it would take a band that could marry all the different facets together – presenting a unique story idea through powerful musical pieces collected together on an album with striking cover. It also helped that the eventual breakthrough came from one of the standout live acts of the era...

The Who

The main songwriting force behind The Who was guitarist, Pete Townshend. He was not only driven by a desire to keep up with the experimentation of his musical peers, but also by religious inspiration - the previous year he'd become a devotee of the Parsi guru, Meher Baba. He later told Mojo magazine: 'I suppose what I wanted was to rescue the pop song which seemed to me to be in serious trouble in the late sixties partly because of the kind of post-psychedelic wetness that seemed to be everywhere. You could write a song that went "Wee love you, Wee love you," and it would get to number four in the charts [a reference to "We Love You" by The Rolling Stones]. I was outraged and desolate because I knew I was too much of a cynic to ever be able to do that. I was a believer in what a group of writers like Ray Davies, Bob Dylan and certain moments in Lennon and McCartney were occasionally uncovering.'

As early as 1965, Townshend was trying to move in a conceptual direction. The first sign of this was the single, 'I'm A Boy,' that had originally been written as part of a science-fiction story called 'Quads' (not related to *Quadrophenia*). The central conceit was that in the future, parents would be able to choose the sex of their children in advance. One couple ask for four daughters, but somehow give birth to a boy so they decide to raise him as a girl nonetheless and he ends up starting a girl-group with his siblings.

Townshend wasn't put off by his failure to complete Quads and made another early foray into narrative work on the nine minute mini-epic, 'A Quick One While He's Away,' which alternated between a number of musical styles in order to tell the story of an extra-marital affair (the track was featured on their second album, *A Quick One*, 1966).

Their next album, *The Who Sell Out* (1967), also featured an extended number in two parts, 'Rael', which was based on

The Who were wild onstage performers, but guitarist Pete Townshend also had literary aims which led to their groundbreaking 'rock opera', *Tommy*. *(Alexander Turnbull Library)*

another of Townshend's plot ideas – it is set in the year 1999 and China is seeking to take over the world and destroy all religions, with their first step being the invasion of Israel (thus giving the piece its title). *The Who Sell Out* also moved further in a conceptual direction by having fake advertisements between each song, in order to poke fun at the growing commoditisation of popular music.

Townshend finally reached his goal of creating a complete dramatic work with *Tommy* (1969) and he coined the phrase 'rock opera' to describe what he was trying to achieve. Townshend was initially daunted by the idea of writing a whole album around a single storyline, so he started out by creating individual songs in embryo and only adjusted them to fit a larger narrative once he had a few that seemed to fit together. The Who's manager, Kit Lambert, was the son of a classical composer and he provided a great deal of encouragement and advice for the project, explaining how the formal elements of opera might help Townshend structure the work as a whole. It was his idea that the album could start with an overture that foreshadowed the musical pieces to come and he also suggested a libretto could be featured in the liner notes so that the overall plot was clearly explained.

This is just as well, since the storyline of *Tommy* is rather convoluted and the work is better understood as a symbolic fairytale, rather than a realistic narrative. The piece begins with Tommy witnessing the murder of his father by his mother's secret lover. He is so traumatised that he becomes deaf, dumb, and blind. This aspect of *Tommy* is meant to represent the way in which people in the modern world are cut-off from their spirituality and thus his journey is a spiritual quest to make himself whole again. Standard medicine cannot help him, so he tries to seek solace in drugs and sex (represented by the 'gypsy acid queen'). His condition means that he is preyed upon by his sadistic cousin and his paedophilic uncle, but he survives these experiences by drawing strength from inside himself and thereby gains a supernatural affinity with the world that allows him to become a champion pinball player.

This bizarre plot twist was added as an at the last minute, after the entire suite was played to the rock critic, Nik Cohn, and he criticised it for being too heavy-handed. Townshend hurriedly wrote 'Pinball Wizard' to lighten the mood and admitted in his biography that this peculiar plot development was equally fraught and necessary: 'I made a huge leap into the absurd when I decided that the hero would play pinball while still deaf, dumb, and blind. It was daft, flawed, and muddled, but also insolent, liberated, and adventurous. I had no doubt whatsoever that [even] if I'd failed to deliver the Who an operatic masterpiece, with "Pinball Wizard" I was giving them something almost as good – a hit.'

After his success as a pinball star, Tommy returns to his hometown as a Christ-like figure and takes over a holiday camp, where his followers gather to hear his teachings (though Tommy is still blind and so the metaphor of the blind leading the blind is clear). His followers eventually abandon him and

Tommy is forced to come to terms with himself, which allows him to regain his sight. Throughout the album, the refrain 'see me, feel me, touch me, heal me' repeatedly arises as a motif and during the finale this becomes a spiritual cry from Tommy, as he grasps for a meaning beyond the world around him.

Many concept albums are driven by a single writer, but Townshend made space for his bandmates to contribute material to the work. Townshend originally struggled to write the songs that deal with Tommy's childhood abuse, since they were inspired by his own mistreatment by his grandmother. John Entwistle (the group's bassist) took over the task, managing to introduce some black humour to the songs ('Cousin Kevin' and 'Uncle Ernie'), which helped the album keep from becoming too morose. Drummer, Keith Moon, suggested the satirical element of having Tommy turn a summer camp into his own religious organisation. Townshend later suggested the album 'would have been the most unbelievably pretentious piece' if it wasn't for the humour that his bandmates introduced.

When it was released, listeners were willing to overlook Tommy's melodramatic storyline and the rawness of Lambert's unskilled production work, because the music was so startlingly fresh and the imaginative vision of the work was so remarkable. It sold around 10 million copies and the band were invited to play at some of the world's most prestigious opera houses: the New York Metropolitan; The Cologne Opera House; and the Theatre of Copenhagen.

Townshend came up with a more ambitious plan as a follow-up, under the working title of *Lifehouse*. The initial storyline described a future in which human beings are all kept alive in pods that keep them in seclusion while the world outside recovers from the ecological damage that their civilisation has caused. This system is kept running by a totalitarian world government that controls the citizenry by feeding them intravenous drugs.

In his autobiography, Townshend explained that the plot was based on his ongoing belief that rock could snap listeners out of their spiritual slumber, though the rulers in *Lifehouse* see this as a dangerous quality: 'Rock music would be quickly identified by the controllers of the grid as problematical, because of its potential to awaken the dormant populace, rock music would be banned. A group of renegades and nerds would set-up a rock concert, experimenting with complex feedback systems between the audience and the musicians, and hack into the grid. People from everywhere would be drawn to the Lifehouse, where each person would sing their own unique song to produce the music of the spheres, a sublime harmony, to become what I called the one perfect note. When the authorities stormed the Lifehouse, everyone would've disappeared into a kind of musical nirvana.'

Townshend and Lambert pitched the piece to Universal Pictures and received US$1 million in financing. The idea was that The Who would perform the piece live and the concert would be filmed, though Townshend also wanted each audience member to be interviewed as they arrived at the venue so that their responses could be used to inspire impromptu elements of the show.

Rehearsals began at a small hall attached to the Old Vic theatre (near Waterloo Bridge in the heart of London). There was an open-door policy, so that people off the street could come and watch, allowing the band to experiment with creating a fully interactive live experience, but this aspect of the plan was its undoing. They had hoped the project would draw in likeminded fans, but instead they got all variety of drifters and troublemakers, including one attendee who climbed onto the stage and verbally abused the band, until he was forcibly removed.

The live sessions were canned and the group re-gathered in the studio to piece the work together. By this stage, Townshend was feeling totally overwhelmed and Lambert was in no state to help him with the project, having overloaded himself with other work (not to mention that he was now in the grasp of a growing drug habit). The concept of *Lifehouse* was abandoned, with some tracks relegated to Townshend's first solo album (*Who Came First*, 1972) and others forming the basis of a resulting album by the band, *Who's Next* (1971). This album still managed sales of four million despite its erratic composition and the Who's next release, *Live At Leeds* (1971), was similarly successful (some cite its pounding drums and blasting power-chords as forming a template for heavy metal).

Townshend regained some of the confidence he had lost and returned to the idea of doing a concept album for their next release. Initially he toyed with writing a musical biography of the Who under the name, *Rock Is Dead*, but eventually decided to take inspiration from fans of the band instead.

In their early years, The Who had been adopted by the newly emerging mod sub-culture and Townshend's working class roots meant that he'd always had an affinity with these fans. Mods were influenced by fashion coming in from Europe, which involved wearing lightly-coloured shirts, blue jeans, styled leather shoes, and sharp cut cardigans. Their predilection for riding Italian scooters often brought them into conflict with motorcycle gangs, who had the 'rocker' look of leather jackets and trousers.

Quadrophenia (1973) was centred around a young mod named Jimmy who was going through a personal crisis as his gang of friends begins to dissolve. He is eventually brought to a psychologist who discovers that he is in fact juggling four distinct personalities within himself. Townshend matched up these personal characteristics with the four members of The Who, with Moon as the lunatic, Entwistle as the romantic, Daltrey as the fighter, and himself as beggar and hypocrite. Jimmy's eventual dissolution leads him to row a boat out to sea, where he ends up marooned on a rocky outcrop, calling out for spiritual enlightenment.

The recording process and subsequent tour created new challenges for the group. Townshend pushed himself in the studio, introducing tape loops, sound effects, and attempting to record the album in quadraphonic sound, whilst also guiding

THE BIRTH OF THE CONCEPT ALBUM

the recording sessions with his bandmates. When they headed out on the road, American audiences had no comprehension of the mod scene and Daltrey fell into long explanations between songs to give some context for how they fit together. The performances also incorporated some of the tape loops and sound effects that Townshend had created, which meant they were at the mercy of technological failures at a few of the early shows. The tour was also a large organisational undertaking, with huge amounts of lighting, PA equipment, and crew required.

Quadrophenia managed to sell over a million copies, but even this impressive figure was well short of their previous two releases. At the time, Townshend saw the band as being in the same position as Jimmy at the end of *Quadrophenia*: '[the album] is about the Who and what happens to us. It starts out in 1965 and ends now, and I left it open-ended on a note of spiritual desperation because we're in the middle of nowhere, not sure where we're going.'

The Who may have been at a crossroads musically, but they were about to make their most audacious move yet. The film director, Ken Russell, had agreed to work with them on turning *Tommy* into a movie. Rather than trying to confine the wild plot into a realistic work, Russell had decided to amp up its theatrical nature and create a work that was just as outrageous and overblown. He arranged for many of the vocal parts to be re-recorded by the main actors, adjusting their delivery to make the piece more like a classic musical. Daltrey took the lead role of Tommy, while the others took background roles (though Moon had a great turn as the paedophilic uncle who is reformed by Tommy and ends up as a pied-piper-like keyboard player, who leads Tommy's cult followers into his camp).

Tommy was an uneven work and much of the imagery now seems overly heavy-handed. For example, when Tina Turner appears as the acid queen, she ends up luring Tommy into a nightmarish man-shaped coffin that injects him with needles. Equally over-the-top is Elton John's role as the 'local lad' who competes with Tommy at the pinball championships (singing the hit, 'Pinball Wizard') and the film veers towards the ridiculous when Eric Clapton turns up as the preacher in a church where parishioners pray to images of Marilyn Monroe and take pills and shots of whiskey as their sacrament.

Despite its faults, *Tommy* was revolutionary in its attempt to bring music to the screen and this wasn't the end of *Tommy*'s reach. It was later turned into a ballet (in Canada), recreated as a synth album (*Electric Tommy*, 1971, by Joe Renzetti & Tony Luisi), and re-recorded by the Who with the London Symphony Orchestra (*Tommy*, 1972) and this latter version also included Rod Stewart, Steve Winwood and Ringo Starr.

Daltrey went on to work with Russell on his next project, *Lisztomania*, which reimagined the composer, Liszt, as a rock star figure (see Chapter Two). Moon followed Daltrey's lead by taking parts in the movies *That'll Be The Day* and its sequel, *Stardust*, while Entwistle occupied himself by recording a pair of solo albums. This left Townshend feeling that his band was no longer interested in backing his more ambitious work and, as a result, the Who's subsequent releases were more standard rock albums.

However, Townshend's most personal work, *Quadophenia* gained a second life when it was used as the basis of a film in 1979. Documentary maker, Franc Roddam, was brought on board as the director and he also co-wrote the script, attempting to connect the loose threads of the album into a more complete plotline. Townshend's character of Jimmy was placed amongst a gang of Mods, who were heading to Brighton to battle with the Rockers. Jimmy was played by Phil Daniels in his first acting role and he gave a gritty portrayal of a young man who lived only for his subculture and couldn't find his way in the wider world. Sting did a nice stint as the coolest 'face' on the Mod scene, though Jimmy's reverence of this character is destroyed when he later discovers him working as a subservient bellhop. This provides a final disillusionment for Jimmy and the film ends with an image of him propelling Sting's character's scooter over the edge of a cliff.

The music of the Who provided an energetic and emotive backdrop for the movie, but their tracks were also placed alongside other tracks that were more reflective of the time when the movie was set (in the mid-60s). The work was a remarkable representation of the Mod movement and the massive gang battles on the beach at Brighton were conducted with such vigour that many of the extras were injured. The resolution of the film was less satisfactory and relied on the mood of the Who track, 'Love Reign O'er Me', to express Jimmy's final mood of spiritual desolation (which worked better on the album than it did on the movie). Despite its downbeat ending, *Quadrophenia* has stood the test of time far better than *Tommy* and has since become a cultural touchpoint for the mod revivalists who emerged in the decades that followed.

Before the filming for *Quadrophenia* had been completed, The Who were hit by tragedy - Moon had choked on his own vomit after a night of heavy drinking and died. Townshend considered closing down the movie, but finally decided that it would provide a fitting testimonial to the band as it had been. The death of Moon effectively brought an end to the Who as a creative entity, though Townshend did initially attempt to keep the group going.

Townshend moved further in a literary direction after this – working as commissioning books editor, releasing a book of short stories in 1985 (*Horse's Neck*), and creating a stage musical from Ted Hughes' *Iron Man* story. He also attempted subsequent conceptual works, most notably the album, *Psychoderelict* (1993), and the mini-opera featured on *Endless Wire* (2006), which were both about a retired musician (Ray High) who is trying to complete his 'Gridlife' project (with the comparison to Townshend and his *Lifehouse* project being made quite clear throughout). *Tommy* made another appearance in 1993, when Townshend was enlisted to help write a new musical theatre version. Despite its faults, *Tommy* remains one of the most well-known and influential albums of all time. It not only popularised the phrase 'concept album' but also inspired many of the artists who would take up this form in the decades to come.

The Kinks

The Kinks emerged at a similar time to the Who and, though they never fully embraced psychedelia, they did join these groups in pushing their subject matter beyond the standard love song and into more peculiar territory.

The group was led by Ray Davies, whose wry social commentaries were well-suited to the changing times. Ray's brother, Dave, was also a songwriter in the group but his work appeared as album tracks or B-sides, which eventually led him to start his own solo career on the side. This led Ray to consider breaking up the Kinks but instead he took even firmer control over the group, writing all of the tracks on *Village Green Preservation Society* (1968) and using his lyrics to write an ode to the traditional English lifestyle (or, at least, Ray's own romanticised version of it).

The Kinks' next release, *Arthur (Or the Decline and Fall of the British Empire)* (1969), carried the theme even further and produced one of their most enduring tracks, 'Victoria' (about the former queen). Ray planned to use the songs as the basis of a one-off television show that was written in collaboration with the young novelist, Julian Mitchell, and the project had the backing of Granada television. In his autobiography (*X-Ray*),

Ray revealed that the work was named after his brother-in-law, Arthur, who had taken his family to Australia: 'I wanted to centre the whole story around an ordinary man like myself, who had been a small cog in the empire and watched it pass him by. After several meetings, I trusted Julian enough to mention my brother-in-law Arthur. We both agreed that he would be an excellent choice, particularly as the name Arthur would also conjure up connections to King Arthur and the Round Table, the Holy Grail, and all that. We were, however, convinced that our story should be about a family that was being torn apart because some of the children were emigrating to Australia. In our scenario Arthur was to be much older, he was to have served in the Great War and it was he who was being left behind in an old world that was in decline.'

The television show was in the early stages of production, when it was abruptly pulled by Granada after they lost faith in the producer running the project. Ray backed away from narrative concepts albums for a few years after this disappointing experience.

The group were also having a tough time for other reasons, as Dave later explained to Mojo magazine: 'There were two main factors to our problems. One, we were banned from working in the States for three years because our manager had fucked up with the unions. And the other was my favourite Kinks album, *Arthur*. I thought we'd really found a path. It felt so right; it was like another "You Really Got Me." Ray was writing fantastic, sensitive words that were so relevant to what was going on –

better than any politician. I was really surprised at the response we got to [the poorly-received single] "Shangri-La", I thought it was going to be a massive hit.'

Fortunately, the group were eventually returned to centre stage by the hit single, 'Lola,' though their managers were unimpressed when they found that the subsequent album, *Lola vs the Powerman* (1970), featured multiple tirades against the music industry and even struck out at the Kinks' management team personally. The band also alienated some of their fans by moving between different musical styles over the next few albums, taking up Americana on *Muswell Hillbillies* (1971) and leaning towards the vaudevillian on *Everybody's In Show Business* (1972).

Ray's next project was even more unexpected – an expansive rock opera that takes the quaint English setting described in *Village Green Preservation Society* and uses it as the backdrop for a battle between two hegemonic leaders. Ray produced so many songs for this project that they ended up being split across *Preservation Act One* (1973) and the double-album *Preservation Act Two* (1974). The former was primarily filled with character studies, while the plot itself was relegated to the second album.

The central figure in the piece was Mr Flash, who has struggled up from a lower-class background to take control of leadership of the government. He is a corrupt politician and cares only for money and shares it only with his inner circle (though he is tough to love if 'Mirror of Love' is to be believed). inner circle are well treated. He is unprepared when Mr Black emerges into the public sphere and gains the public's support with a more puritanical vision of how the country should be run. At first, Mr Flash is simply battling for his own skin, but gradually it becomes clear to him (and the listener) that there is more at stake – while Mr Black portrays himself as a more trustworthy political force, he actually wants to introduce a totalitarian regime that will be far worse than what preceded it. But Mr Flash's realisation comes too late. Mr Black's repressive regime takes over the country, using brainwashing to force dissidents to join their cause, and the piece ends with the 'happy' citizens singing the praises of the new society they have created.

During the production of *Preservation Act One*, Ray was through a personal crisis - his wife had left him and later won a court case to retain custody of their two daughters. Ray took it very badly, downing enough valium and alcohol to end up in hospital. This caused no interruption in the band's touring schedule and Ray began taking a steady diet of uppers (prescribed to him by his doctor) so he could continue to perform each night. He spent one concert, popping so many of these pills that he emptied the entire container. At the end of the show, he tried to announce the end of the band, but the P.A. had already been shut-off and instead he collapsed backstage, once again ending the night with a trip to the hospital's emergency room.

This briefly delayed the release of *Preservation Act One*, but the band continued on regardless. Dave later admitted in his autobiography that he felt entirely disconnected from the band's creative process by this stage: 'I was beginning to get frustrated and bored with Ray's concept ideas. I really wanted to get back to playing straight ahead rock'n'roll again.'

It didn't help that the band's album sales were also steadily declining. Ray was unperturbed and returned to the idea of producing a television show for Granada. This time it would be a thirty-minute musical play called *Starmaker*. Ray took the role of a rock star who wanted to take over the life of a normal working man (Norman), so he could write a song that would capture the hopes and dreams of an average person. As the show went on, it was revealed that we are actually seeing the daydreams of Norman himself, who falsely imagined that he was a rock star in disguise rather than just a normal person living a relatively boring life.

The piece was filmed in front of a live audience and Ray made light of this fact by directing questions directly to the audience, as well as finally going out to sit amongst them once Norman realises that he is an everyday person after all. Meanwhile, the rest of the band were unimpressed to find themselves relegated to the role of a backing band and their presence was only pushed to the fore in the last song, when Norman gets up to dance amongst the audience and leaves aside his star aspirations. The songs from the piece were released on *A Soap Opera* (1975). By this time, Ray had already moved onto his next project, *Schoolboys In Disgrace* (1975), which captured he and his brother's troubles at school (Dave had been expelled, as had their sister). This album is also tied into Ray's earlier work by a suggestion in the liner notes that the protagonist is a Mr Flash in his youth.

The Kinks' career was also given new life by a high-profile record deal with Arista and the fact that Van Halen had just had a hit in the US with their early single, 'You Really Got Me.' During recording sessions for their next album, Ray told Phonograph Record that his conceptual days were now behind him: 'I've been trying to tell too much of a story, trying to make things relate as an overall work instead of trying to make each song work. The songs are better now without a concept.'

The Kinks instead returned to the classic songwriting that had originally made them famous. Their individual concept albums failed to have the same ongoing resonance as *Tommy*, but their overall thematic interest in 'Britishness' provided an inspiration for later artists from the U.K., including Blur (see Chapter Six).

Expanding Beyond Psychedelia

Whilst *Preservation Act Two* might've resonated with the other concept albums of their era, the Kinks' other works over this period had been too down-to-earth to fit with the tripped-out visions of their musical contemporaries and their conceptual works were eventually overshadowed by their catalogue of hit singles (meaning their role in the history of concept albums is often overlooked). Instead, the psychedelic era was best exemplified by the Who's *Tommy*, which took rock into the realm of opera and showed that an album could be novelistic in scope. The scale of this endeavour no doubt influenced the prog musicians, who were next to adopt the concept album. They would also up the ante by using the form to inspire complex musical compositions and outrageous live performances.

Chapter Two

The Arrival of Prog

The desire to expand the range of popular music that had emerged in the sixties didn't just die away once the decade came to an end, though some of the most innovative musicians did move away from the social commentary of The Who and The Kinks, and focused instead on their music's compositional aspects. This would see the emergence of the genre that is most often related to concept albums: Progressive (or 'Prog') Rock.

Despite the perceived connection between prog and conceptual material, many of its proponents only carried their themes across single album sides or within long, extended musical pieces, rather than doing complete concept albums. Their interest in the form took it to new levels of popularity, while also drawing criticism for replacing the raw emotion of rock'n'roll with a more studied, pretentious approach – a criticism that dog concept albums for decades afterward.

Many of the foremost prog musicians had experience in classical music and wanted to invest rock with more depth and musical complexity, creating a form of popular music that took on the entire history of European composition and the innovations of modern jazz. Their music was experimental but in a highly structured manner which moved between different time signatures and musical keys, though they did sometimes incorporate the type of noisy free-jams that had been popular with avant-garde psychedelic groups such as The Grateful Dead.

The new musical movement started in England in the late 60s with the arrival of King Crimson. Their debut release, *In The Court of the Crimson King* (1969), wasn't clearly conceptual, but their first four albums were written around the central elements of life: Air, Water, Fire, and Earth. King Crimson were a favourite of music critics and their album hit number five on the UK charts only six months after their first show. However the group's fiendishly intricate music limited their ability to follow-up this early success, though they laid the groundwork for the next few groups we shall look at. The band's declining popular audience meant they were soon haemorrhaging members and one of these was singer/guitarist Greg Lake, who hung around long enough to contribute to King Crimson's next release, *In the Wake of Poseidon* (1970). Lake then took up the bass as his primary instrument and put his energy into a new project, Emerson, Lake and Palmer (ELP).

His new songwriting partner, Keith Emerson, was already known for using classical compositions as inspiration for his previous group, The Nice, which helped give birth to the sub-genre of 'symphonic rock' (as did the work of the Moody Blues). Emerson was known for playing blistering solos on his state-of-the-art Hammond organ and stunned audiences by stabbing knives between the keys when he wanted to hold down a note. The ELP line-up was rounded out by drummer, Carl Palmer, who'd previously played in the short-lived, bizarrely-dressed group, The Crazy World of Arthur Brown. He was hardly a shy performer and at the height of ELP's career, he had a purpose-built drumkit made for him, which could rotate 360° while he was playing.

ELP moved into conceptual work on their breakthrough second album, *Tarkus* (1971), which propelled them to fame on both sides of the Atlantic. The album had a gatefold sleeve, which provided a large canvas for their cover designer, William Neal, to work upon. The frontpiece showed 'Tarkus' – an armadillo which had tank tracks instead of legs – and the interior artwork showed the creature emerging from an egg, then battling with three other part-robot animals, before being stung in the eye by a manticore (an animal from Greek mythology) and retreating into the sea. Emerson later explained that they were presenting 'a reversal of how life is supposed to have begun on the planet. It's evolution in reverse after the final nuclear explosion.'

The imagery on the cover matched up loosely with the lyrics on the conceptual side of the album. Lake wrote 'Stones of Years' as a comment on the failure of the human race to realise the 'stupidity of conflict'; while 'Mass' was about the hypocrisy of religious nations going to war. The track, 'Battlefield', then concluded the piece by showing that the result of war is only destruction.

It was hardly a strong conceptual statement when examined closely, but ELP nonetheless did provide inspiration for later creators of concept albums in the way that they took the imagery from their album onto the live stage. A huge model of the Tarkus was created, which was able to produce jets of foam from its mouth that would float out toward the audience. However Palmer found that the prop did occasionally cause difficulties, especially during one show in Brighton: 'we had it aimed in the wrong direction, and it poured all this stuff straight out into the grand piano! Filled it up! We had to stop the show, and on came the roadies with dustpans and the hoover to clear it up.'

Attempts to create models from the other Tarkus illustrations were equally fraught. The flying creature looked particularly ungainly as it hung on a wire overhead and was eventually cut from the show. The parade of onstage creatures were matched by the increasing size of the band's own gear: Emerson was dwarfed onstage by an immense stack of keyboards and Palmer had a steel drumkit that was backed by two enormous gongs, as well as an overhead monastery bell.

They followed this with a more adventurous project - a live rendition of *Pictures At An Exhibition*, a classical piece by Russian composer, Modest Pertrovich Mussorgsky (1839-81). The central melody was kept close to the original notation, though the rock format gave it a pulsing, energetic drive. Once again, William Neal provided a cover design and introduced sci-fi and fantasy elements to the 'pictures' that related to each movement of the piece

A couple of albums later, they returned to the idea of doing a long conceptual piece. *Brain Salad Surgery* (1973) featured 'Karn Evil 9', which was over thirty minutes in length and had to be started at the end of the first side of the album so the entire composition would fit. The lyrics were written in collaboration with Peter Sinfield (who'd previously worked with Lake in King Crimson) and the album art was done by H.R. Giger (known for his work on the *Alien* films).

In the years that followed, it was *Tarkus* that came to be remembered as ELP's most enduring conceptual work, despite the fact that 'Karn Evil 9' was actually ten minutes longer in duration. It is a testament to ELP's efforts to marry the artwork, lyrics and live representation of their Tarkus piece that this has become their defining work. In actual fact, their final album, *Love Beach* (1978) also featured a twenty-minute long narrative piece ('Memoirs of an Officer and a Gentleman'), but it was a rather dull effort that centred on a soldier in World War Two reminiscing about the woman he has left behind.

During the preceding years, Emerson had pushed for ELP to tour with a full orchestra, though this sapped tour revenues, eventually putting the band three million dollars into the red. *Love Beach* was intended to reinvigorate the band's fortunes, but it was a dismal failure and their fading fortunes eventually wore down the group's morale and, by the end of 1978, they had decided to go their separate ways.

Yes and Rick Wakeman

Yes took things even further than ELP by attempting to spread a single piece across a whole double-album on their much-loved and much-maligned magnum opus, *Tales of Topographic Oceans* (1972). Yes came out of the same musical scene as ELP and the two groups used the same producer, Eddie Offord, for their early albums. Yes started as a more conventional psychedelic rock group but moved in the direction of prog around the same time as King Crimson. The two core figures in the group were Jon Anderson (singer) and Chris Squire (bassist), and the pair's obsessive quest to advance their music saw them cycling through a cast of bandmates during their early years. However if we look at Yes in terms of concept albums then the most important member of the group was keyboard virtuoso, Rick Wakeman.

Rick Wakeman began playing piano at age six and by age ten he was winning prizes in competition with much older children. In his final years of high school, his attention was drawn toward rock 'n' roll and he joined a number of working cover bands in his area, before becoming a session musician. He would go on to record with Lou Reed, Cat Stevens (on 'Morning Has Broken'), Elton John, Cilla Black, and Marc Bolan. However, his most striking contribution in his early days was the warped mellotron line on the David Bowie classic, 'Space Oddity.' Bowie was so impressed with Wakeman's work that he hired him to record all the keyboard parts for his subsequent album, *Hunky Dory* (1971).

In the meantime, Wakeman had been admitted to London's most prestigious music institute, the Royal College of Music. He managed to fit his studies around his work as a session musician for two years, before finally quitting to join The Strawbs. They helped put Wakeman in the public eye, but their folk leanings didn't leave much room for him to express his true talents, even after they made the move to electrified instruments. He began looking for other opportunities and soon found himself being courted by both David Bowie and Yes. Bowie wanted him to help with the recording of *Ziggy Stardust and the Spiders from Mars* (1972, see Chapter Three) and to become a touring member of his band. Wakeman was tempted, but instead took up the offer to join Yes, since it was promised that he would be a full contributing member of the band (as opposed to being just one of Bowie's backing group).

Wakeman's first album with the group, *Fragile* (1972), was a massive hit and established them as the foremost prog group. The album had a number of short, throwaway pieces that helped make it accessible to the casual listener and the opening track, 'Roundabout', was trimmed to half its length so it could be released as a single (hitting 13 on the US charts). Yet Anderson and Squire were seeking a greater challenge and pushed the group towards increasingly dense compositions, with alternating rhythmic dynamics and key signatures. Their next album, *Close To The Edge* (1972), consisted of only three extended pieces and provided a stake in the ground, marking the point at which listeners either followed Yes deeper into the musical unknown or wrote off their musical experiments as pompous self-indulgence. For many, the whole enterprise of progressive rock went against the freewheeling spirit of rock'n'roll, but this criticism did little to dissuade Yes from making an even more extravagant statement on their next album.

When the group returned to the studio, the individual members worked to create bewilderingly complex musical passages, which were then stitched together to create four side-long tracks. Wakeman's input provided invaluable since he brought in compositional techniques from his classical training to structure the four pieces as a single masterwork and he suggested the introduction of repeating motifs that would hold the separate elements together. Nonetheless, the resulting double album, *Tales From Topographic Oceans*, was one of the most impenetrable rock albums to ever be released. It didn't help that Anderson had taken the lyrics from a book of Indian sutras and these layered another level of convolution to what was already a challenging listening experience.

Yes had a firm following at home and were just making their first inroads overseas, which meant that they had to keep up a heavy touring and recording schedule. Despite all these commitments, Wakeman found himself with creative ideas to spare and squeezed in time to record his own solo album, *The Six Wives of Henry VIII* (1973). Given full rein for the first time, Wakeman had produced an instrumental concept album that had a song for each of the ill-fated wives of the historical king. Yes' record company were aghast, but they didn't want to upset a key member of one of their most popular acts so they arranged for a limited release of the album, accompanied by only minimal promotion. Much to their chagrin, it went on to sell six million copies over the following five years.

Wakeman was bolstered by this success and became interested in the idea of using his grounding in classical music to create music that straddled the middle ground between rock and opera (thereby advancing the 'symphonic rock' approach taken by the Moody Blues, The Nice, and ELP). His next move in this direction was taking part in a live performance of The Who's *Tommy*, along with the London Symphony Orchestra. Here he would make some useful contacts: the producer, Lou Reisner; and composers, Danny Beckerman and Will Malone.

Rick Wakeman being interviewed by a journalist in a *Journey to The End of the Earth* T-shirt. *(Bruce Jarvis)*

All three of these collaborators were enlisted for his next project, *Journey to the Centre of the Earth* (1974) a stage version of Jules Verne's book of the same name, written for rock band, choir, and orchestra. In some respects, this composition sat halfway between a musical and a concept album since it was primarily written for the stage and English actor David Hemmings (who'd starred in Antonioni's film, *Blow-up*) was brought in to narrate the piece (though it didn't have actors for each part, so was unlike a musical in this sense).

Wakeman still took a central place during the performances, looking oddly elfish with his shoulder-length blonde hair and dressed in flowing white robes. His core band consisted of musicians that he regularly jammed with at a pub near his house, though they were dwarfed during the live performances by three tiers of choir singers at the rear of the stage and the full orchestra that sat alongside them. Tickets for the concert series sold out so quickly that the producers neglected to put any comps aside for Wakeman's family and he was forced to buy some back from a tout at an extortionate price (the tout took pity on him and threw in a few free tickets for the football Cup Final).

As soon as the shows had been completed, Wakeman hurried to mix the live recordings so that he could release them as an album to cover debts incurred by the live shows, but his record company remained sceptical about his potential as a solo artist and wouldn't even commit to releasing it. At the last minute, Wakeman's manager managed to get the tapes to the company's president, Jerry Moss, in California and he signed off on the release.

When it came time for Wakeman to turn his attention back toward Yes, he found that he was no longer interested in following them down the rabbit hole of musical abstraction and, during one show, he became so bored that he arranged for a roadie to order him a curry, which he ate onstage during sections where the keyboard parts were minimal. The other members of Yes were nonetheless shocked when Wakeman announced his departure.

Interestingly, Yes originally considered replacing Wakeman with Vangelis Papathanassiou, who later dropped his surname and gained fame as a film composer (writing scores for *Blade Runner* and *Chariots of Fire*). Anderson had been impressed by an album that Vangelis had released while a member of Aphrodite's Child – a concept album called *666* (1971), about the last days of man, as described in Revelation. Yet, Vangelis only took part in a few practices with the group before deciding it wasn't for him.

Wakeman's decision to leave Yes was justified a few weeks later when *Journey to the Centre of the Earth* hit the top spot in the UK album charts. Wakeman had only just turned twenty-five but he had achieved more than most people would in a lifetime. Unfortunately, his fast-paced achievements had also been matched with a lifestyle of heavy drinking and chain-smoking and, as he was preparing to set out on a tour in support of the album, he was struck down by a heart attack.

It took over four weeks in the hospital for Wakeman to recover, during which time he worked on the basic framework for his next album: *The Myths and Legends of King Arthur and the Knights of the Round Table* (1975). He wanted to do a release show at the Wembley Empire Pool, but the preceding dates were booked for an ice skating event so the middle section would be iced over. Wakeman was unperturbed and simply worked the ice into his stage-plan. A giant castle was constructed in the centre and professional ice skaters were hired from around the world to take part.

The show was a great promotional ploy, but it was hugely expensive and even selling out three nights in a row didn't save the project from running at a loss. Worse still, it was Wakeman's own money that had financed the venture and the main response from the press was scorn and derision. In his autobiography, Wakeman recalled this period as being one of his lowest periods: 'I honestly wondered at one stage if it would be the last record I would ever make.'

Wakeman was relieved when he was given a composition job on the film, *Lisztomania*. The director, Ken Russell, had previously released the immensely successful film adaptation of *Tommy* so he'd been given free rein to take his next work into even more ludicrous territory. He enlisted Roger Daltrey as Liszt and Ringo Starr as the pope, while Wakeman himself was given a smaller part as a Frankenstein-like creature given the name of 'Thor.' The plot re-wrote history by portraying Liszt as a rock star figure, who battles to save the world from Wagner's plan to steal Liszt's melodies and use their power to create a new race of super-humans. If this wasn't peculiar enough, the film also featured multiple dream-sequences, one of which showed Daltrey with a giant prosthetic penis which was drawn into a guillotine between his Russian lover's legs. Needless to say, the film was nearly unwatchable and it remains as one of the most extravagant failures of seventies film.

When Wakeman met with his manager to plan for his next album, he was given the news that the record company would no longer finance his overblown epics and wanted him to return to recording with a straightforward rock band. Wakeman had no choice but to do as they requested, since he was already in the position of having to sell his house. Wakeman's reign as the king of the concept album was over. His next solo work, *No Earthly Connection* (1976), still racked up 3 million sales but his live audience steadily declined from this point, as people realised that he now delivered only a standard rock show. He eventually returned to Yes, who had also moved toward the mainstream and it wouldn't be until the eighties that Wakeman would attempt another themed work (see Chapter Four).

Wakeman's work was further proof that concept albums could be commercially viable, even when they moved far beyond the bounds of standard rock music. His live shows were even more astounding, showing that conceptual works could work on a large scale. ELP might've stunned audience with their use of stage props, but Wakeman pushed it to the limit with dozens of musicians onstage for his *Journey To The Centre of the Earth* shows and playing in the midst of an ice skating rink for *The Myths and Legends of King Arthur*.

The next act that we'll look at was also driven to bring their concept album to life on the live stage, though their budgets never reached the heights of Wakeman's. Instead they used film projections and stage trickery to bring their surreal artistic vision to life.

Genesis

Genesis were another English group that were interested in reaching beyond the usual limitations of rock. Few of the groups mentioned above were comfortable with being classified as 'prog' acts, but Genesis were the most adamant about not being given this label. Nonetheless, just like the groups mentioned above, they delved into a number of longer works, starting with 'Supper's Ready' a twenty-two minute long mini-epic that filled one half of their album, *Foxtrot* (1972). The lyrics are as abstract as anything written by any of their prog contemporaries, but seem to be about a couple undertaking a spiritual journey that ends with them viewing the biblical apocalypse from the Book of Revelation (the track broke new ground by featuring one of the earliest examples on a rock album of the guitar technique known as 'finger-tapping'). Their lead singer, Peter Gabriel, tried to infuse their live shows with extra meaning by dressing in elaborate costumes and incorporating special effects, such as levitating above the stage with the aid of thin wire cables.

When they first attempted a concept album, *The Lamb Lies Down On Broadway* (1974), their guitarist Mike Rutherford actually believed it would help the group break free from being labelled as a prog group: 'People think we're more airy fairy than Yes or ELP but I've never thought we've been at all like those bands and I think this ... album will end those comparisons forever. The most important things to us is the songs – we're not as concerned with flaunting musicianship. It's our most direct album – although the songs are related, they stand up separately.'

The creation of the album was contentious from the start and Rutherford was more interested in the idea of attempting a musical retelling of the children's short story, *The Little Prince* (by Antoine de Saint Exupéry). Gabriel eventually won over his bandmates and they began work on his project. However, he was soon distracted from the writing process by an offer he'd received from the filmmaker, William Friedkin (who'd previously worked on *The Exorcist* and *The French Connection*). The director had been impressed by the narrative ideas in some of Gabriel's songs and wanted to talk to him about collaborating on a movie. This project came to nothing, though Friedkin retained his interest in working with popular musicians and a few years later he enlisted synth instrumentalists, Tangerine Dream, to score his film, *Sorcerer*.

The recording of *The Lamb* was also interrupted when there were medical complications with Gabriel's wife's pregnancy, which drew him away to the hospital. These repeated distractions caused some friction within the band, especially when Gabriel continued to insist that he should write all the lyrics for the album himself, meaning that his absence effectively stalled any progress. It also didn't help that he'd written a plot that his bandmates barely understood so they only had a limited ability to contribute their own ideas.

Gabriel was inspired by his observations of New York during a short tour of the U.S. The steam rising up from the grates in the sidewalk gave him the idea that there might be an underworld beneath the street. He created a fictional character to explore this underworld, using the last two syllables of his own names to create the name, 'Rael.'

He later explained to his biographer, Chris Welch, that the character was a complete fabrication: 'Rael is half Puerto Rican and lives in New York and he'd be the last person to like Genesis! I've yet to talk to the genuine article but that's not important. He's alienated in an aggressive situation. The Lamb arrives on Broadway and acts like a catalyst. A very oppressive sky descends over the city and solidifies. It becomes a screen like a TV with the camera behind it. Real life is projected on the screen and starts to break up. It's rather like the Victorian's reaction to early photography. The screen that Rael sees is sucking him in. When he regains consciousness he is in another underworld.'

Rael is searching for his missing brother, John, but first he has to face an increasingly bizarre array of creatures and situations. He is initially trapped in a cocoon, then a cage of stalagmites, before reaching a room of 'carpet crawlers' who tell him he must choose one of the thirty-two doors ahead in order to find a way out. He hears a woman crying off to one side and goes to comfort her. She tells him that the next door is actually a seat that he needs to sit upon. More unearthly creatures come upon him - a 'supernatural anaesthetist' (who is a stand-in for suicide), the lamia (a pool of snake-women) who are poisoned by trying to drink his blood, and the 'the slippermen' – creatures with bulbous protuberances that cause them to be obsessed by every physical sensation. Rael finds that John is also amongst the slippermen and discovers that their only chance of escape is through being castrated. Just when Rael seems to have found his way back to Broadway, he is drawn back by a vision of his brother drowning.

Suddenly he realises that John is a figment of his imagination and he has been actually searching for a lost part of himself. This final realisation brings Rael together with 'IT', though Gabriel avoided explaining this concept or the exact meaning of the work as whole: 'It's quite a barrage of words. There should be an award for people who go through it! But I'm a great believer in mumble-jumble sense. I prefer things to give an air of meaning, rather than meaning itself. You can't look for meaning in some of the lyrics, they just present an atmosphere … The story is printed on the sleeve because it was too encompassing for all the songs to contain the action – it's a clothesline on which you can hang up the songs.'

The weakest parts of the album result from Gabriel trying too hard to work his lyrics into a poetic form. 'The Arrival' begins by taking a line from Wordsworth ('I wandered lonely as a cloud'), but quickly descends into ungainly phrases, such as: 'with nonchalant embracing/each orifice disgracing.' Some events in the narrative also seem tacked-on, as when Rael has a hallucination of a factory and there is a somewhat randomly-introduced critique of production in a capitalist society ('The Grand Parade of Lifeless Packaging').

The many complex strands of *The Lamb* meant that it was a difficult sell to the listening public and it only managed moderate sales in the UK. During the subsequent world tour, Gabriel tried to inject elements of the storyline into the live show by dressing as Rael - putting on a leather jacket and using facial make-up to darken his skin. There were also three projection screens at the rear of the stage, which showed 1450 slides (projected by seven projectors), each image relating to a moment in the story. Rael's eventual realisation that he is searching for part of himself was portrayed by using a lifelike dummy that had been modelled directly on Gabriel (even to the point of using a plaster-cast of his face to create the head). The lights would go down to darkness and then suddenly Gabriel would appear centre-stage, facing an exact image of himself.

The other members of Genesis were shunted to the back of the stage and began to feel that Gabriel's routines were taking over the whole show (just as the other members of the Kinks had felt during Ray Davies' *Starmaker* project). His bandmates' scorn for these fanciful performance pieces also spread to the tour's road-crew, who began to play tricks on the singer by toying with his stage-double. On one occasion, a banana was left hanging out of the fly of the dummy's trousers and, on another, one of the roadies shocked Gabriel by unexpectedly taking the dummy's place. Gabriel was devastated by the

The Lamb Lies Down On Broadway by Genesis - the cover showed the main character, Rael, staring at three images of himself. (*Hypgnosis*)

division he was causing and, halfway through the tour, he told their manager that he'd decided to leave the group to start a solo career.

Gabriel was eventually replaced on vocals by the group's drummer, Phil Collins, and the group moved into more accessible musical territory. Given the progressive nature of their early work, it is amazing to note how smoothly they managed to reinvent themselves as a chart-topping pop act. Yet this was nothing compared to the astonishing success that both Phil Collins and Peter Gabriel had as solo performers in the 1980s. Nonetheless, the group members retained a love for their early work and there were even discussions about re-staging *The Lamb* as a stage show in the new millennium. This didn't eventuate, but the album stands as a testament to the eccentric ambitiousness that Genesis showed in their early years.

Other Early Prog Conceptual Works

Jethro Tull were another group who were labelled as a prog act, though their music was initially rooted in the blues and jazz. The band were led by singer/flautist, Ian Anderson, whose abstract lyrics often made it difficult to nail down the subject matter of his songs and this caused some misunderstandings of what he was trying to achieve.

Many took *Aqualung* (1971) to be an album-length meditation on the problems of organised religion, but Anderson was horrified to find the work being labelled as a concept album and reacted by using the band's next release to supply the critics with exactly what they seemed to be looking for – a completely oblique conceptual statement. The band were reticent about revealing this agenda to the public at the time, but Anderson later admitted as much in an interview that was featured on the 1998 edition of the album: 'The *Aqualung* album had generally been perceived as a concept album, whereas to me it was just a bunch of songs ... So the first thing about *Thick As A Brick* was – let's come up with something that is the mother of all concept albums and really is a mind-boggler, in terms of, what was then, relatively complex music. And also lyrically was complex, confusing and, above all, a bit of a spoof. It was – in a nice way – tongue in cheek and meant to send up ourselves, the music critics, and the audience, but not necessarily in that order.'

Thick As A Brick (1972) featured a single, album-length track that was supposedly based on a poem written by a twelve-year old boy named Gerald Bostock. The arguments about the subject matter of this piece continue to this day, filling discussion boards with a multitude of interpretations, with many taking it simply as a mockery of the whole prog enterprise.

In any case, Jethro Tull's desire to toy with the idea of the concept album does show that working with this form was a mixed blessing – many critics and audience members were fascinated by albums that seemed to have a secret meaning or difficult to interpret story beneath them. At the same time, there was a pretension in trying to fulfil this expectation. Jethro Tull struck a middle ground by keeping their concepts vague and leaving it to their fans to decipher them as much or as little as they wished.

There was certainly the outline of a plot on their next album, *A Passion Play* (1973), which followed 'Ronnie Pilgrim' in a journey through the afterlife. Yet the band shied away from presenting it as a serious spiritual journey by having their bass player break into a comedy routine in the midst of the album and by presenting the fantastical elements as humdrum – for example, Lucifer is renamed 'Lucy' and Pilgrim reviews his life by watching a film version of it.

Music critics weren't impressed with the game that Jethro Tull were playing and it received decidedly average reviews. This led them to produce a more standard effort, *War Child* (1974), though even the songs on this piece do seem to revolve around the central theme of violence (once again, the dense, poetic lyrics make it difficult to say this with any confidence).

Whether Jethro Tull's albums should be taken as coherent concept albums remains unclear, though it's certainly true that fans of the group had a high time trying to decipher a coded message within them.

There was more obvious intent behind the narrative pieces released by Canadian prog act, Rush. The band never went as far as stretching a narrative over an entire album, but they did have three records in a row that featured side-long conceptual pieces. They moved in this direction after Neil Peart joined as

Ian Anderson from Jethro Tull toyed with his audience's expectation of what a concept album should be. *(Bruce Jarvis)*

their drummer in 1974 and took over writing the group's lyrics, taking influences from science fiction and fantasy novels.

'The Fountain of Lamneth' on *Caress of Steel* (1975) was a twenty-minute track (divided into six parts) about a quest to find a mythical fountain. Unfortunately, the group were still learning to gel as a musical unit and the album came off as a patchy affair, despite the incredible musicianship that the three-piece displayed. Their record label encouraged them to return to their roots in hard rock, but the group were still convinced they could carry off a conceptual piece.

Peart created a clearer storyline for the title track of their next album, *2112* (1976). His lyrics described a future civilisation where all knowledge is controlled by Priests of the Temples of Syrinx. The protagonist of the piece finds a guitar that allows him to tap into another form of expression, but when he tells his fellow citizens about this wonderful discovery, he is reported to the priests and they destroy the guitar. He ultimately decides to commit suicide rather than live under their repressive regime. This plot has echoes of The Who's *Lifehouse* project, but the album liner notes state that its actual inspiration came from a short story written by Ayn Rand (a mid-century philosopher, who believed in self-reliance and individualism). The coherence of '2112' was cemented by having no gaps between the seven tracks that made up the plot and it remains the most accessible of Rush's conceptual pieces.

Rush's innovative music and unusual subject matter gradually caught the ear of adventurous listeners, especially when FM radio DJs began to pick up on the group's work. It took five years, but *2112* eventually hit platinum sales in the US and even their derided album, *Caress of Steel*, managed to achieve gold status (though it took until 1993).

Their next album, *Hemispheres* (1978) featured their final multi-song epic, 'Cygnus X-1, Book II: Hemispheres,' which followed a space traveller's journey through a black hole and into the mythological land of the Greek gods, Olympus. What happens from this point onwards is anyone's guess, though there is apparently a 'battle of heart and mind' and the space traveller is proclaimed as 'Cygnus, the God of balance' for his ability to find an equilibrium between these two forces. The music that accompanies this tale is equally audacious and it ranks alongside *Tales of Topographic Oceans* as one of the most intricate compositions to emerge from the prog era.

The strain of producing the piece was enough to discourage the group from attempting further conceptual work and Peart's lyrics gradually took on more realistic subject matter. Their fanbase continued to grow and the band went on to become the most successful rock group that Canada has ever spawned.

Prog's Association With Concept Albums

The early prog rock scene has been seen as a golden age for concept albums. Yet only a few of the works mentioned above actually went beyond a single album side. Others were held together by musical and lyrical themes that were hard to decipher and this made it difficult for listeners to fully appreciate them – certainly this was a limitation of Yes' *Tales From Topographic Oceans*. In fact, the work of their rejected keyboard player, Rick Wakeman, probably contributed more to the advancement of the concept album. Ironically, Genesis may have rejected the 'prog' moniker, but actually produced one of the most expansive and thoroughly articulated concept albums of this period with *The Lamb Lies Down On Broadway*.

Prog's association with concept albums had both a positive and negative effect on how they were viewed. From this point onward, there would be a sense that creating a concept album was a pretentious endeavour that went against the original intent of rock'n'roll as a wild, carefree musical style. At the same time, prog musicians greatly expanded the possibilities of the album format through their effort to tie together all the elements of their creative output. The lyrics and the music were used to generate stunning album art and this imagery was also used to inspire elaborate live shows that went far beyond just a set of musicians standing on a bare stage.

The musical complexity of prog had less influence (at least, until the prog metal movement of the following decade), but many subsequent acts picked up on its use of new sounds and fantastical imagery. As we will see in the next two chapters, this emphasis on bringing album imagery alive on stage would go on to be a trademark of seventies rock.

Chapter Three

Concepts of the Future, Concepts of the Past

Prog rock aficionados were not the only seventies musicians interested in expanding the imaginative scope of their records. Concept albums were still a fresh phenomenon and afforded a chance to explore the new ideas that had arisen in the previous decade. Musicians from the varied genres of rock, funk, and country music saw that they could stir up interest in their work by basing it around a central theme or storyline.

The previous decade had also been a time of great technological advance, symbolised most fully by the televised coverage of the first man walking on the moon and there'd been huge strides when it came to issues of racism and sexism. At the same time, the counter culture's dream of social revolution was beginning to fade – the Vietnam war had continued despite the endless protests and the egalitarian society envisioned by the hippie movement failed to materialise.

David Bowie picked up on both these elements – his 'Ziggy Stardust' persona reflected the growing interest in space travel and science fiction, while his album, *Diamond Dogs*, looked into the future through a dystopian lens, inspired by the rundown urban centres that he passed through on tour.

Funk group, Parliament, were also inspired by the changing times. They had lived through the emancipation of African Americans, but saw that the task was only half-completed. Rather than responding with earnest political tracks, they wrote upbeat, good time music that pictured space-travelling African Americans who'd come to earth to save humanity. Despite their use of humour, the underlying pro-black sentiment was clear. Unlike the prog groups, neither Bowie nor Parliament used complex song structures to make their work seem forward-looking and instead gave their music a fresh feel by focusing on futuristic themes and matching this with upfront use of synthesisers (which were still a relatively new invention).

Meanwhile, there was another current of concept albums that reacted to the changing times by looking back to the past. Primarily these were albums by U.S. country acts, who wanted to connect their work to the tradition of American roots music and show that the hippies weren't the only ones who could create musical tales to attract the youth of the time. But before we look at these musicians who delved into the past, let's look at those who looked toward the future...

David Bowie

David Bowie originally emerged during the heyday of the psychedelic era, with his first, self-titled album arriving in 1967.

His songs were initially folky numbers that occasionally drifted into the surreal but, after a few albums, he moved toward fifties rock'n'roll and took up the image of a glitter-clad rock star, following in the footsteps of Marc Bolan (T-Rex). Together they heralded in a new generation of rockers that wore shiny jumpsuits, applied make-up like war paint, and adopted provocative bi-sexual affectations.

Bowie created a new persona, 'Ziggy Stardust,' so that he could take the glam style to a new extreme. The name was inspired by two sources: 'Stardust' was taken from a much-derided artist who had been on the same record label as him, 'The Legendary Stardust Cowboy'; while 'Ziggy' was the name of a tailor's shop that happened to catch Bowie's eye. The latter connection was fitting since Bowie believed that a musical star is made as much through image and fashion as they are through music.

Ziggy was to be portrayed as an extraterrestrial rock star, whose great fame was followed by a heady decline. Bowie had plenty of examples to draw from in the preceding couple of years, during which Jimi Hendrix, Jim Morrison, Janis Joplin, and Brian Jones had all died young. Bowie was particularly intrigued by the mental disintegration of pop star Vince Taylor, whose final show Bowie had attended: '[Taylor] came out on stage in white robes and said that the whole thing about rock had been a lie, that in fact he was Jesus Christ – and it was the end of Vince, his career and everything else. It was his story which really became one of the essential elements of Ziggy and his world-view.'

As a result, many of the songs on *Ziggy Stardust and the Spiders from Mars* (1972) focus on the concept of stardom ('Lady Stardust', 'Star', 'Hang On To Yourself'), while there are only a couple that directly refer to the idea of a rock star from outer space. However, it is possible to read other album tracks as fitting with the theme by seeing them as songs that Ziggy might have played (in fact, often during his live sets, Bowie would introduce 'Moonage Daydream' as being a song written by Ziggy). The remaining tracks add very little to the album's concept, even if they fit stylistically because of their underpinning in 50s rock tropes – especially tracks such as 'It Ain't Easy' and 'Suffragette City' (which Bowie had originally written for Mott the Hoople, rather than intending it specifically for the *Ziggy Stardust* album). Despite the haphazard nature of the album's construction, it was given its power as a conceptual piece by Bowie's decision to fully inhabit the character of Ziggy Stardust.

At the time, Bowie's manager, Tony DeFries, had convinced him that to be a star all you had to do was start acting like one, so he'd began to travel regularly in limousines and hired a personal bodyguard. Bowie realised that by taking on the role of an extraterrestrial rock star, he could exaggerate the otherworldly nature of the pop idol, whilst also imbuing the album with a sense of mystique and drama. He dyed his hair bright red, after seeing a magazine spread by designer, Kansai

Yamamoto, which fitted the models with wigs from Japanese kabuki theatre. To get his hair to stand up like the wigs, Bowie applied layers of lacquer and then blow-dried it until it held firm.

Bowie also took on the androgynous nature of Ziggy and told interviewers that he was bisexual. Gay activists in the UK were buoyed by having such a popular artist come out publicly and it also gained him a lot of press coverage (though it hampered his progress in the US market). Bowie later distanced himself from his claims to be bisexual and, in the end, it seems that his original statements may have been a testament to how much Ziggy had seeped into his own life, rather than being a reflection of his true sexuality.

As the legend of Ziggy Stardust continued to grow in his mind, Bowie contemplated turning the work into a musical or television show. These ideas were eventually abandoned, though Bowie did present his proposed ending to Rolling Stone magazine: 'Ziggy is advised in a dream by the infinites to write the coming of a starman so he writes "Starman," which is the first news of hope that the people have heard. So they latch on to it immediately. The starman that he is talking about are called the infinites, and they are black-hole jumpers. Ziggy has been talking about this amazing spaceman that will be coming down to save the earth. They arrive somewhere in Greenwich Village ... The end comes when the infinites arrive. They are really a black hole, but I've made them people because it would be very hard to explain a black hole on stage ... When the infinites arrive, they take bits of Ziggy to make themselves real because in their original state they are anti-matter and they can't exist.'

Music writer, Nicolas Pegg, has pointed out that this final element of the plot may have been taken from a Doctor Who television special that aired not long before work on Ziggy Stardust began. The idea of Ziggy as a messianic rock star figure also has a similarity to The Who's *Tommy*, though Bowie's vision for the final plot twist was even more fatalistic – it eventually turns out that the aliens are simply using Ziggy as a vessel to mislead the Earth's population in preparation for an invasion and the story ends with his final descent into madness and the destruction of the earth.

Bowie's next album, *Aladdin Sane* (1973), also allowed him to take on a fictional persona, though on this occasion there was no sense of a narrative underlying the character and instead Bowie drew more directly on his own experiences. His half-brother, Terry, had suffered from schizophrenia and first inspired the song name. Bowie then decided to use the name to capture a new, Ziggy-like character, which he could use to reflect upon his previous year undertaking long tours around the US. In this respect, it was Bowie himself who was becoming 'a lad insane' as he struggled to balance his need to be a flamboyant rock star at night, while retaining some personal space to be himself during the day. *Aladdin Sane* is too vague in its themes to be considered a concept album, though it certainly kept the Bowie mythology alive, while he searched for his next big idea.

Following the *Aladdin Sane* tour, Bowie again turned his mind to writing songs around a more structured narrative. His initial idea was to write a work based on George Orwell's novel, *1984*, but the writer's widow refused to give her permission for the project. Nonetheless, Bowie incorporated some ideas from the book into his own dystopian vision: 'I had in my mind this kind of half Wild Boys / *1984* world, and there were these ragamuffins, but they were a bit more violent than ragamuffins. I guess they staggered through from *Clockwork Orange* too. They'd taken over this barren city, this city that was falling apart. They'd been able to break into windows of jewellers and things, so they'd dressed themselves up in furs and diamonds ... So these were these gangs of ... roller-skating, vicious hoods, with Bowie knives and furs on, and they were all skinny because they hadn't eaten enough, and they all had funny-coloured hair. In a way, it was a precursor to the punk thing; that's the way it was going. That was what I decided would be my rock musical, *Diamond Dogs*. It never came up to being a rock musical, but I got damn near it.'

Bowie's vision of an urban centre that has fallen into ruin was drawn from his recent trips through the Eastern Bloc, where the modern tower blocks built in the sixties were already beginning to look like decaying monoliths and he'd also noticed the growing social degradation in the urban centres of New York and London, which suggested these cities might follow suit.

Another inspiration was his father's work with Dr Barnado's Homes for orphans, which was an organisation that had been started by Thomas Barnado in the late 1880s. In particular, Bowie's imagination was sparked by the idea that Barnado had found some orphans were living on the rooftops in London.

The opening track of *Diamond Dogs* sets the scene with a narrated description of a city where 'fleas the size of rats sucked on rats the size of cats.' The title track follows on from this theme and the next three songs run together as one unit – Sweet Thing, Candidate, and Sweet Thing (Reprise). The final four tracks are also thematically linked and are all drawn from Bowie's interest in *1984*. The title of 'We Are The Dead' is what Orwell's main characters said to one another when the 'thought police' came to break them up, while there is an even clearer vision of Bowie's original inspiration on '1984' and 'Big Brother'. The album ends with 'Chant of the Ever Circling Skeletal Family', which seems to suggest the collapse of society and a descent of humans back into the wild. It is an oddly unnerving piece, which falls into a lurching 5/4 time signature and fades out with a repeated tape loop of Bowie repeating the word 'brother' with its final syllable clipped off.

At the centre of the album, the theme seems to loosen with 'Rebel Rebel' (originally written for the stage version of *Ziggy*) and the ballad, 'Rock 'n' Roll With Me'. For a lesser artist, these tracks would've weakened the overall statement, but the strength of Bowie's vision was strong enough that the listener felt compelled to fit them into the overall logic of the album.

Once again, Bowie's embodiment of the theme was a powerful factor, especially on the cover art which shows him with the hind-quarters of a dog, staring fixedly toward the viewer. For the live shows, Bowie took up the role of 'Halloween Jack' from the title song, described as a 'real cool cat who lives on top of Manhattan Chase.'

Diamond Dogs was as close as Bowie ever came to writing songs of social commentary and in the booklet of the 30th anniversary edition, he admitted that the political theme was purposefully kept below the surface: 'This album again has a theme. It's a backward look at the sixties and seventies and a very political album. My protest. These days you have to be more subtle about protesting than before. You can't preach at people any more. You have to adopt a position of almost indifference. You have to be supercool nowadays. This album is more me than anything that might be in my imagination.'

Diamond Dogs may have had a deeper meaning, but it certainly wasn't trying to change the path of society. The optimism of the sixties had faded like a puff of marijuana smoke and the psychedelic dreams of a better world had turned out to be just that. Bowie's own drug of choice was cocaine, a habit that left him looking increasingly gaunt and eventually led him to the dark visions of *Station to Station* (1976). Bowie later revealed that this album was in fact driven by a central set of themes, even if his description of how these connected together was rather vague: 'the words themselves, "station to station", have a significance inasmuch as they do refer to the

Stations of the Cross, but then I took that further through the Tree of Life. [The album] had a certain magnetism that one associates with spells. There's a certain charismatic quality about the music ... that really eats into you.'

Bowie's next three albums – *Low* (1977), *Heroes* (1977), and *Lodger* (1979 - are often referred to as a trilogy and were all influenced by the involvement of Brian Eno (an experimental musician who had started his career in Roxy Music). This move would take Bowie away from concept albums and he felt the change in approach gave him a new enthusiasm for his work, saying at the time: '[Eno] got me off narration, which I was so intolerably bored with.' It wasn't until the nineties that Bowie returned to the idea of doing a concept album (see Chapter Six).

Parliament/Funkadelic

The other great musical purveyors of futuristic musical visions in the seventies came from a starkly different background than Bowie. Parliament and Funkadelic were two funk groups that revolved around the band leader, George Clinton. Both groups used science fiction imagery to present a futuristic vision of African Americans as space travelling super-heroes, though Parliament's work provided the clearest representation of Clinton's over-riding vision. By using sci-fi imagery, Clinton managed to promote African American empowerment while investing his work with wild flights of fancy and a great deal of humour.

CONCEPTS OF THE FUTURE, CONCEPTS OF THE PAST

A number of funk artists prior to this had also created work that was based around central concepts. Marvin Gaye's album, *What's Going On* (1971), took on a number of environmental and political issues, which made it feel like a single statement piece. A similarly cohesive work was Stevie Wonder's album, *Innervisions* (1973). The opening track, 'Just Enough For The City' describes a struggling family in Mississippi and this eventually sees the son moving to the rough streets of New York. This song provides a strong curtain-raiser for an album that portrays the troubles of modern urban life – the struggles to find work and the disconnection with spirituality that city-life engenders. However, it was Parliament that would present the most fully-imagined narrative in their work and they also took the same level of imaginative brio into their live shows, which were packed with strange costumes and larger than life props.

The 'Parliaments' were originally a doo-wop group formed by barbershop owner, George Clinton. A disagreement with his record label, coupled with his growing interest in funk music saw him take up the name Funkadelic. Even once Clinton regained rights to the name 'Parliament', he decided to keep the two groups running as separate entities – Funkadelic became his outlet for psychedelic-rock influenced funk, while Parliament took a more soulful approach. Nonetheless, the distinction between the groups became less noticeable over the years that followed and they eventually combined under the name, 'P-Funk.'

George Clinton followed in the footsteps of James Brown in

CONCEPT ALBUMS

George Clinton is regarded as a funk music legend, but his playful conceptual works also deserve recognition. *(Garry Brandon)*

creating a phenomenal live band, bringing on board flamboyant musicians such as Bootsy Collins (bass) and Bernie Worrell (keys). Clinton wanted to show that funk could be just as outrageous as prog or glam rock by presenting a future in which outer space is travelled by African American astronauts and all issues of racial prejudice are long-forgotten.

The underlying storyline that Clinton used as inspiration was introduced on *Mothership Connection* (1975), where we first meet the 'Starchild' who has come down from the mothership to bring the freeing power of funk. A more complete mythology was given on the intro to their next album, *The Clones of Dr Funkenstein* (1976), during which we are also introduced to Starchild's original mentor, Dr Funkenstein, who originally discovered the life-giving properties of funk. The 'Prelude' begins in the form of a fairy-tale ('funk upon a time') and describes a time when 'funk flowed freely and was free from the need to be free.' But dictators took over the lands and repressed space aboard the mothership, leaving the secret of clone funk hidden deep inside the Egyptian pyramids. Now it has become the people, forcing the 'Thumpasorus Peoples' to escape into safe for them to return and bring musical emancipation to the Cro-Nasal Sapiens.

The outlandish humour of this storyline masked the fact that there was also a serious side to Clinton's vision. He recognised that science fiction was a genre dominated by white culture, so he appropriated it and twisted it to his own needs, creating a mythology for African Americans to replace the cultural history that'd been robbed from them by the slave trade. He plays on the original meaning of 'funk' as a bad smell, suggesting that it is now an essential life-force, which only switched on people can pick up. This explains why the people who were left-behind are called 'cro-nasal' and also why the name of Starchild's nemesis is Sir Nose D'Voidoffunk.

Funkentelechy Vs. the Placebo Syndrome, (1977) introduced this new character and the term 'funkentelechy' which mashed together the words: funk, intellect, and technology. Starchild defeats D'Voidoffunk by using a bop-gun to 'funkatize' him, effectively forcing him to dance to the groove of their music (the cover shows these two characters, with Starchild holding the bop-gun).

Listening to individual tracks from Parliament albums of this period, it would be easy to overlook the thematic element to them, since all the talk about bringing the funk comes off as a simple exhortation to groove. Yet Clinton ensured that the metaphorical elements of his work were given life in the band's live shows, which included a large model of a spaceship that was lowered onto the stage during the track, 'Mothership Connection.' The band themselves grew to be a massive ensemble and members took to wearing flamboyant costumes to differentiate themselves from the throng of musicians.

Eventually the scale of the project became unsustainable, causing Parliament/Funkadelic to splinter into smaller outfits. Parliament had a last hit single with 'Atomic Dog' in 1984 and then Clinton directed his focus towards recording occasional solo albums and producing work by other artists (most notably, the Red Hot Chilli Peppers album *Freaky Styley*, 1985).

The legacy of Parliament can be seen in the conceptual elements introduced by other African American artists during the eighties. The ambitiousness of Clinton is echoed by Prince, who used his music as the basis for three films (the most successful being *Purple Rain*). The political aspect of Parliament also helped inspire the ambitiousness of the early Public Enemy releases (see Chapter Six) and this group took up the approach of presenting themselves onstage as a large unified collective.

More importantly for our current purposes, Clinton showed that the concept album didn't have to be pretentious and rigidly performed, it could be just as effective when used to produce work that was humorous and funky. His work doesn't spring to mind when one thinks of conceptual works and this is probably because there is no specific album that can be pointed to as a crystallisation of his narrative ideas. Nonetheless, the collective impression left by his sci-fi pieces is far clearer than that presented by some of the more esoteric and well-known prog works, so it seems justified to list his name amongst the pioneers of the concept album in the seventies.

Country Music

Country music has always had a storytelling tradition, though usually each tale is only carried out within a single song. It is also a genre that often draws material from the history of the American West, using the same subject matter that has fed a plethora of pulp novels and movies. One might see Woody Guthrie's album, *Dustbowl Ballads* (1940) as a precursor to the Country concept album, though Johnny Cash's *Ballads of the True West* (1965) and Lee Hazlewood's *Trouble is a Lonesome Town* (1963) were more representative of the albums that would follow (given that they were based in the 'Wild West'). In the early seventies, this approach was taken up by a new generation of musicians.

The social upheaval that set David Bowie and George Clinton looking into the future, provided country and folk artists with an equally strong impulse to rediscover the traditions of the musical forbearers. Rather than trying to adopt a new sound, these artists took up traditional forms and tried to find a new path forward from these original sources. Along with these musical forms came an interest in the stories of the past and these artists began to introduce a sense of history into their work as a way to find a new grounding for it.

Certainly this is one way to understand *Babbacombe Lee* (1971) by English folk act, Fairport Convention. The band were initially inspired by the electrified folk and country rock scene in the US, but also drew from the traditional music of the British Isles. *Babbacombe Lee* told the true story of a condemned man from the Victorian era. The songs were run together in long sections that told the different chapters of his life – he originally worked in the Royal Navy, but was injured and then employed by Emma Keyse, who he was later convicted of murdering (on slim evidence). The gallows failed three times in a row and so he was imprisoned instead of hanged and finally released many years later. The songs were blended into long sections that weren't given separate titles, which encouraged listeners to consider the piece as a complete work.

Meanwhile, across the Atlantic, US groups were also looking to the past to seek new inspiration. This was essentially a continuation of the experiments in roots music that was started by the US folk movement and eventually came to country music through the work of Bob Dylan and the Byrds. The scene took up a new life in California and it was here that The Eagles emerged as a central act. Two of the members – Glenn Frey and Don Henley – had already toured as members of Linda Ronstadt's band, while Bernie Leadon had been in the Flying Burrito Brothers and Randy Meisner had been in Poco. The quartet took the feel of country music and turned it into classic rock.

For the second Eagles album, *Desperado* (1973), Henley had the idea that they could retell the story of cowboy outlaws, the Doolin-Dalton gang. A couple of the songs were co-written with country rock legend, Jackson Browne (who'd previously co-written their hit 'Take It Easy'), though it was the title track written by Henley and Frey that went on to be one of the band's signature tracks.

Aside from the opening/closing track ('Doolin-Dalton'), it would be easy to listen to the album without realising there is a theme at play, but once this context is taken into account, the listening experience becomes much richer. The early tracks like 'Twenty-One' and 'Out Of Control' provide a sense of a youthful danger, which then lead to the song 'Outlaw Man' at the centre of the album.

Similarly, if you took 'Desperado' on its own, it would seem to have little to connect it to outlaw cowboys apart from its title, but in fact the theme of choosing love over money runs throughout the album (though in the lyrics, this is phrased in terms of choosing the Queen of Hearts over the Queen of Diamonds). The song's relevance is made clearer in the reprise version at the end of the album, where it is combined into a medley with the 'Doolin-Dalton' track from the start of the album. This finale track is preceded by 'Bitter Creek' which was actually the nickname of one of the members of Daltin-Doolin

Glen Frey (left) and Don Henley (right) co-wrote songs for *Desperado*, but it was Henley's idea to theme it on the Dalton-Doolin Gang. *(Bruce Jarvis)*

gang and this song sets the stage with the narrator saying: 'We're going to hit the road for one last time / We can walk right in and steal them blind.'

Then 'Doolin-Daltin/Desperado' paints the picture of Bill Doolin being shot down and refers to how 'The Queen of Diamonds let you down,' before returning to the main refrain of 'Desperado.' Given the central importance of this track to the album, it makes sense that 'Desperado' went on to be a signature tune for the group, though it wasn't even released as a single at the time. However, it's real success as a song came when it was covered successively by Linda Ronstadt, The Carpenters, and Kenny Rogers. The album itself was also a breakthrough release for the group, proving how powerful their mix of country music and modern rock could be and it went on to sell over two million copies.

Country legend, Willie Nelson, also achieved one of his greatest successes through a conceptual work. *The Redheaded Stranger* (1975) told the story of a preacher who kills his wife and her lover after finding them together. At first it seems he has been set on a path of violence, but he gradually comes to terms with the evil that he has done and starts a new life.

Nelson spent many years trying to gain backing from one of the large movie studios to make the piece into a film, but was finally forced to secure private funding. The film was eventually released in 1986 and took the same title as the album, with Nelson doing a decent job in the lead role. Yet the movie would never match the success of the album which continues to be considered as one of Nelson's finest.

Songwriter-turned-singer, Randy Newman, didn't actually play country music as such, but nonetheless took on the myth of the cowboy on his album *Good Old Boys*. (1974), which took the listener from the traditional country lifestyle described on 'Louisiana 1927' through to a biting critique of the modern Southern man on 'Rednecks'. The songs not only examined the backward attitudes that he saw around him, but also the unfair liberal view that all Southerners were racist. Its concept may have been loose, but it was a remarkable political statement, making it an interesting juxtaposition to the political albums of Stevie Wonder and Marvin Gaye which had been released in the preceding years.

Unsurprisingly, the idea of doing a concept album about the life of a musician was also picked up within country music. Emmylou Harris had often used her sister's name, 'Sally,' as a pseudonym when checking into hotels and she began to jokingly refer to herself and her band as 'Sally Rose and the Rosebuds.' This idea grew in her mind and she began writing songs about this fictional character, though wasn't sure if she would have enough pieces for an entire album.

In order to complete the work, she brought in the English songwriter, Paul Kennerley, who had already recorded two concept albums of his own – *White Mansions* (1978) about the US Civil War and *The Legend of Jesse James* (1980), which featured both Harris and Johnny Cash. *The Ballad of Sally Rose* (1985) told the story of a young female musician, who falls in love with an older man ('The Singer'), who gives her an apprenticeship in songwriting and eventually falls in love with her. When Sally begins to be more successful than her lover, she leaves for the city and he begins drinking heavily to cope with his feelings of loss and failure. Yet she decides that she cannot live without him and decides to return to his arms, only to find that he has died in a car-crash. She vows to continue playing and begins recording his songs as a way to keep his legacy alive.

Many commentators picked up on the similarity to Harris' own relationship with Gram Parsons, though she would only admit to being partially inspired by those events. The album re-energized Harris' career and helped clear the way forward: 'It was kind of frightening. But also, I was at the point where there were so many things I needed to change about my life and the thing that was pulling me toward the change, and the project that was sort of my crowbar, was *Sally Rose*.'

Harris began to perform the entire album at every live show, before returning to her hits and this cemented the work in the hearts of her fans. The tour was very successful and Paul Kennerley eventually became her third husband.

Overall, the run of country albums discussed above seem like an overlooked vein of conceptual work. It may be that the more brash efforts of Bowie, Parliament, and the prog movement simply left a more outrageous and unforgettable image in the public's shared memory. However, it is clear that country music also had its conceptual era, which produced some equally timeless musical works.

The Spread of the Concept Album

The artists in this chapter may still seem as if they have more differences between them than similarities, but their work reflects how concept albums can be used by a songwriter to reflect upon the changing circumstances of the world around them. For Parliament and David Bowie, this meant looking into the future, while many of the country artists tried to reassess their place in the modern world by looking into the past. However, the tradition of the country concept album slowly faded after this, while Parliament and Bowie's influence continued to grow.

One of Bowie's key breakthroughs was that he had realised that if he took on the role of a fictional character then he could bring his vision to life without having to didactically connect each song to the central narrative. This aspect of role-playing created a mythology around his work and gave his concept albums a sense of coherence, even when the songs were only tentatively linked. This no doubt helped inspire similar approaches by artists as diverse as Kiss (see Chapter Five), Deltron 3030 (see Chapter Six), and My Chemical Romance (see Chapter Seven).

Bowie and Parliament also stunned audiences of the time with their ability to apply their musical concepts to their live shows. Next we will turn our attention to a group that took this approach to its inevitable extreme. It's time to turn our attention to Pink Floyd.

Chapter Four

Pink Floyd & the Legacy of Prog

Pink Floyd are the only band in this book who could warrant having the majority of a chapter to themselves. Their career spanned the movements of psychedelic music and prog, and they incorporated elements of each as they progressed towards their own unique sound. They also took all the showmanship of prog to the live stage, combining this with the theatrical drama of David Bowie and the hulking stage props of Parliament to create a show that dwarfed those of their contemporaries (and this was no mean feat in the age of Kiss, see Chapter Five). Their album artwork also became an integral part of how the group presented their work and the main cover images often became motifs for the band.

The arrival of punk music in the late seventies may have seemed to announce the death knell of prog rock, but in fact this coincided with Pink Floyd's most impressive conceptual effort, *The Wall* (1980), which proved that high-minded musical endeavours could still find an audience in an era of back-to-basics rock.

Pink Floyd

Pink Floyd made their name by playing long, free-form psychedelic jams, but their ongoing success was also due to their ability to infuse their music with a melodic core that had none of the glaring atonality of other experimental forms of the time (such as free jazz or contemporary classical music). It no doubt helped that the group had a grounding in rhythm and blues, which was the form of music that brought them together as students (most of the members were enrolled in either architecture or fine arts). This formative influence is reflected in the fact that their name is a homage to two underground blues players – Pink Anderson and Floyd Council.

The group's original lead singer, Syd Barrett, was drawn toward the steadily growing counter-culture and his experiments with LSD encouraged him to write tracks that had purposefully open sections to allow for improvisation. These provided the perfect fit for the 'happenings' that were taking place in the city and Pink Floyd's shows were often accompanied by slide projections and homemade lighting effects. One of these events was attended by Paul McCartney, who'd disguised himself as an Arab for the night and their influence can be heard in the noisy crescendo of 'A Day In the Life.'

Barrett also proved himself to be adept at writing quirky pop hits and Pink Floyd scored two early hits with 'Arnold Layne' and 'See Emily Play.' Their first album, *Piper At the Gates of*

Dawn (1967), was more reflective of their experimental live sound and set the path for the albums that followed. Barrett himself would soon drop out of the band - his growing psychological problems made him withdrawn and incommunicative, and he'd become a liability during live shows (if he could even be found). On a number of occasions, the band's roadies had to be sent back to the previous night's accommodation to retrieve items (money, his guitar) that he'd left behind in his room. The band's bass player, Roger Waters, eventually decided they needed to find another guitarist/singer to take Barrett's place and he chose David Gilmour, a childhood friend of Barrett who had shared his interest in guitar playing during their teenage years.

Waters also took over writing lyrics for the group and their music began to rely on sparse, drifting melodies that were occasionally offset by moments in which the music gained pace and introduced winding rock solos. Their ethereal music was perfect for film scores and they composed pieces for Antonioni's film *Zabrickie Point* and the French film *La Vallée* (which produced the album, *Obscured by Clouds*, 1972).

The band's talents came to fruition on *Dark Side of the Moon* (1973). The songs were more accessible than on the group's previous releases, though the music still showed an interest in experimentation and the single, 'Money,' became a worldwide hit despite being written in the off-kilter time signature of 7/4. In the studio, the band made use of newly developed synth keyboards and reversed tape loops to provide a fresh sound to their music.

The album was also their first attempt at using a unifying theme to tie together the songs as whole. Waters asked his bandmates to list the most important issues in their lives and came up with a list of subjects: death, money, religion, and madness. Waters used these as a starting point for writing about contemporary society, though his lyrics still betrayed the influence of sixties idealism, especially on the anti-war song 'Us and Them' and on 'Money,' which parodied the materialistic lifestyle of the rich.

The album cover was created by design company, Hipgnosis, who had also worked on a number of the band's previous releases. The band members were presented with a range of choices, but quickly gravitated toward the bold image of light rays hitting a triangular prism being separated into the main elements of the colour spectrum. The use of the triangle was a reference to the Egyptian Pyramids as an ultimate symbol of man's desire to show off his own power. Waters saw the cover as an effective way of tying together metaphorical imagery that ran through his lyrics: 'The album used the sun and the moon as symbols: the light and the dark; the good and the bad; the life force as opposed to the death force.'

Waters came up with the idea of also tying the tracks together by using short snippets of people speaking about the themes of madness, violence, and death. He wrote a set of question cards and then recorded short interviews with anyone he could find around the studio, including the band's roadies, bouncers, and their partners. Wings were recording at the studio next door so he also taped an interview with Paul McCartney, along with his wife Linda and their guitarist, Henry McCullough. However only McCullough's quote was used on the final recording since the others sounded too forced. The resulting dialogue segments made repeated references to madness: 'I've been mad for fucking years – absolutely years'; 'I've always been mad, I know I've been mad, like most of us have.' This was a theme that would echo through much of Pink Floyd's work following Syd's departure

Music fans across the world were taken by the band's ability to combine innovative, futuristic sounds with classic songwriting and the album was a smash hit – going on to become one of the biggest selling albums of all time. Its conceptual basis may not have been obvious to many of those who bought the album, but the thematic coherence of the songs does give it a grand feel and propels it toward the crescendo of its final track, 'Eclipse.'

Pink Floyd were also a hugely popular live act and their interest in putting on an impressive light-show meant that they now travelled with a couple of articulated trucks full of equipment. At one set of shows in London's Earl's Court, a full-scale model of a Spitfire fighter plane was strung up on rigging that reached back to the rear of the auditorium. The plane then swooped over the audience during the final song, before reaching the stage in an explosion of light and sound.

The success of *Dark Side of the Moon* may have made things more financially comfortable for the group, but it had the opposite effect on their creative drive. Their relentless tour schedule had left them feeling exhausted and there was a huge expectation for their next album to match up to the success of its predecessor. Waters decided that he'd draw directly from this experience on their next work. He wanted to make a statement about the darker side of success in the music industry and his starting point was the decline of Syd Barrett, which he addressed on the track, 'Shine On (You Crazy Diamond).' The intro of the song was built around a melancholy guitar line that Gilmour had come up with, which reflected the long shadow that Barrett's decline had cast over the group. The song set the mood for their next album, *Wish You Were Here* (1975) and Waters saw that by splitting the song in two and placing it at either end of the album, he could provide a structure for the work as a whole.

Ironically, Barrett actually turned up to the studio during the recording sessions but initially no one recognised him since the skinny young man that they had known had now morphed into a sixteen-stone man, with only a few wisps of hair on his head. His former bandmates rebuffed his offers to record some guitar parts, though they allowed him to stay and observe the recording process. He sat agitatedly in the control booth, occasionally rising to brush his teeth with a toothbrush that he kept in his pocket. His appearance added a layer of poignancy to the sessions and perhaps contributed to the sense of melancholy that permeated through the track that they wrote as a tribute to him.

Elsewhere on the album, Waters' emotions turned from sadness to disdain as his focus shifted to the music industry. He described 'Welcome to the Machine' as being about 'them and us and anyone who gets involved in the media process.' While 'Have a Cigar' was constructed from comments he'd overheard being made by music industry execs. The dark mood of the album partly reflected the infighting that was occurring behind the scenes. A feeling of claustrophobia had settled on the group after spending so long in close proximity and small events, like a person arriving late to the recording session, could explode into a passionate screaming match. As a result, Pink Floyd only did a brief tour in support of *Wish You Were Here* and then took time off to recuperate.

When they returned to the studio to record *Animals* (1977), the internal dynamics of the band were as fraught as ever. The band's keyboardist, Richard Wright, was going through a bad divorce, so had little energy to put into the recording. Over the past three albums, Waters had gained confidence as a singer and simultaneously moved to the centre of the group. He now began to squeeze the others out of the creative process, bringing him into conflict with Gilmour. The band's next two albums would be strong conceptual statements by Waters and his singlemindness would end up alienating his bandmates in a way that was clearly reminiscent of what had happened for Ray

Davies (see Chapter One) and Peter Gabriel (see Chapter Two) when they moved in a similar direction.

Animals (1977) took its inspiration from George Orwell's novel, *Animal Farm*, but instead of critiquing Communism, the songs used the metaphor of farmyard animals to criticise capitalism. The pigs represented the rich who controlled society, the dogs were the police and military who kept order, while the sheep were the remaining masses of docile consumers. As a political statement, it was fairly trite and four of the album's five tracks were monolithic in structure – not only long, but with moody, expansive instrumental sections. None of the tracks were suitable radio singles, but their sheer scale made them an enigmatic listening experience for their serious fans.

Hipgnosis were again brought in to create the artwork, but this time Waters had his own idea of what was required. He'd been walking by the River Thames and had been struck by the imposing Battersea Power Station - a huge industrial brick building, which had large smoke stacks rising from each of its four corners. His idea was to commission a gigantic inflatable pig and then photograph it flying in the skies overhead. Hipgnosis arranged for a German Zeppelin manufacturer (Balloon Fabrik) to create a huge pig balloon, but it was so large that during the first attempt to launch it, the crew ran out of helium to fill it and had to push the shoot back by a day. Early the next morning, the pig finally took to the sky. The photographer took pictures from a distance so the flying pig was perfectly captured passing through the front two smoke stacks of the Battersea Power Station, like a ball floating between two goal posts.

Suddenly a gust of wind ripped apart one of the guide ropes and the crew on the ground lost control. Not long afterward, an airline pilot coming into land at Heathrow reported that he had seen a large pig-shaped balloon floating below the cloud cover. A police helicopter was sent up to keep an eye on its flight path and they kept it in sight until it reached above 5000 feet. Radar operators followed its progress to around 18,000 feet, before losing track of it somewhere over Kent. The deflated pink beast was discovered in a field a few days later.

The resulting press coverage was a boon for Pink Floyd. They had another blow-up pig constructed, this time with a glowing set of eyes, and it was inflated at the side of the stage during their live show. It was an impressive sight, but the gimmicky nature of the pig was something that began to play on Waters' nerves. He had written an album criticising capitalism and yet his band had become a huge money-making machine, which now played colossal stadium shows and whose members all lived in audacious country houses. What's more, his audience didn't seem interested in his attempts to invest his music with meaning; they only wanted to hear the hits.

Near the end of one show at Montreal's Olympic Stadium, Waters became so disheartened by hearing the crowd calling for them to play 'Money' that he ended up spitting on an audience member who'd been screaming at him from the front row.

Reflecting on what had happened, Waters came to realise that success was now a barrier that stopped him from being able to communicate with their fans through his music and the idea came to his mind of creating a literal wall between the audience and the band.

Band unity was at an all-time low by this stage and they'd made the decision to become tax exiles in France, hoping to save money after the machinations of their financial advisors had seen them lose a million pounds (with tax still to pay). It was propitious timing since the music scene in London seemed to be turning against the group's lofty, overblown compositions towards a more direct approach. Punk had arrived and heralded a return to short, sharp songs delivered with aggressive energy. The attitude of this new movement was captured by a widely printed photograph of Johnny Rotten wearing a t-shirt emblazoned with 'I Hate Pink Floyd.' Nonetheless, Pink Floyd's drummer, Nick Mason, embraced the scene by producing an album for The Damned, while Gilmour and Wright focused on recording solo albums.

Waters felt as if he was the only one who was now contributing worthwhile material to Pink Floyd and so he came up with an overarching concept for the next album, which would leave little room for the others to get involved. The work followed the life of a fictional musician (named 'Pink Floyd') whose trajectory followed Waters' own biography.

The story began with Pink's life as a child during the Second World War, then jumped forward to his life as a touring rock

David Gilmour and Nick Mason with a huge inflatable pig that was part of Pink Floyd's live shows well into the eighties. *(Garry Brandon)*

musician. The idolisation of the rock star was taken to extremes by having Pink morph into a fascist leader. Waters later explained to Mojo magazine how this unusual story arc grew from a couple of central ideas: 'Initially I had two images — of building a wall across the stage, and of the sadomasochistic relationship between audience and band, the idea of an audience being bombed and the ones being blown to pieces applauding the loudest because they're the centre of action, even as victims. There is something macabre and a bit worrying about that relationship — that we will provide a PA system so loud that it can damage you and that you will fight to sit right in front of it so you can be damaged as much as possible — which is where the idea of Pink metamorphosed into a Nazi demagogue began to generate from.'

The album begins with Pink's childhood and the news that his father has died in World War II (as Waters' own father had done). The first metaphorical 'wall' is the protective shield his mother creates between him and the outside world. Pink is also alienated by his experiences at school, where the harshness of the teachers leant towards sadism.

The story then skips forward to show Pink as a hedonistic rock star, whose success creates another wall around him, distancing him further from the outside world. Waters once again made direct reference to Syd Barrett - especially in lines such as: 'I've got elastic bands holding my shoes on, I've got a bag with a toothbrush and a comb' and 'I've got wild, staring eyes.' The album is also a very personal reflection on how his own success as a musician had left him disconnected from his audience and those around him. On the song, 'Comfortably Numb,' Waters makes reference to one show that he played after taking heavy-duty painkillers, which left him feeling as if his 'hands were as big as two balloons.' He captures his own unease with crowd mentality by having Pink slowly morph into the leader of a fascist group, turning his fans into violent thugs for his cause. The finale of the album sees Pink being put on trial for his sins, though it ends with an image of psychological release with the wall between himself and the outside world finally being torn down.

Waters' interest in fascism has many resonances with the work of Ray Davies on *Preservation Act Two* – both songwriters recognised the messianic appeal of the 'rock star' and fed this into their storylines. We can see both the attraction of the freewheeling lifestyle (as led by Pink as a rock star and Mr. Flash) and the opposing rigid lifestyle (as represented by Pink's turn to fascism and Mr. Black's rise to power). It is striking how similar the speeches of Pink and Mr Black end up sounding, showing that both Waters and Davies were haunted by the evil shadow cast by Nazi Germany in the early years of their lives.

The bold vision of the project was enough to keep Gilmour on board, though he later explained to Mojo magazine that he thought *The Wall* betrayed an overly negative aspect of Water's personality: 'it was Roger listing all the things that can turn a person into an isolated human being. I came to see it as one of the luckiest people in the world issuing a catalogue of abuse and bile against people who'd never done anything to him ... There was some good music in it, although frankly I think the rest of us felt some of it wasn't quite up to standard ... Things had always been a bit rocky. We worked very well together, but we were never the closest of friends.'

For his part, Waters now saw himself as holding sole responsibility for writing music for the group and he considered his main collaborator on *The Wall* to be the producer, Bob Ezrin, rather than any of his bandmates. He considered Wright's contribution to be near non-existent and hence insisted that he should leave the group after the tour to promote the album, otherwise Waters threatened to take the master tapes and release them as a solo work. This would have meant that Wright would receive no money for his work so far and he was still deeply in debt from his divorce the year before, which had coincided with the band's more general financial problems.

Despite the growing friction within the group, their career was about to hit its second peak of success. The lead single 'Another Brick In The Wall' seemed to resonate with dissatisfied teenagers everywhere, with its chorus proclaiming 'we don't need no education, we don't need no thought control.' Many teachers across the UK were unimpressed and poured scorn not only on Waters, but also the London school teacher who allowed his class to sing on the original recording. Waters reacted by explaining that the song was only meant to reflect his own childhood experience, rather than be a rejection of the education system as it currently existed. Despite the bitterness of the song's message, it actually provided one of the only elements of humour on what was for the most part a gloomy and melancholic collection of songs.

The Wall went on to sell 20 million units across the world, making it one of the darkest albums to achieve such a level of worldwide popularity. In comparison, *Never Mind The Bollocks* (1979) by the Sex Pistols only reached sales of half-a-million (as calculated by Rolling Stone magazine in 2003). Clearly the punks hadn't been as successful as they'd hoped in wiping prog off the face of the earth.

The live show that accompanied *The Wall* was so expensive to stage that it was only performed in four cities: London, Los Angeles, New York, and Germany. For a number of years, the band had been using the animations of painter, Gerald Scarfe, to provide backdrops for their live show and this time he outdid himself, creating warped images of Pink's vicious school teacher and overbearing mother. These were used as models to create huge inflatables for the live show and Scarfe also created animations that could be projected on a screen above the band during their performance. Pink's infatuation with fascism was represented by a symbol of two hammers laid across one another, which came to life in Scarfe's animations and began to march in line. As the show went on, the stage-crew layered up massive fake bricks made from cardboard along the front of the stage until the band was entirely obscured from view. The finale involved these bricks collapsing, while lighting effects and fireworks were used to mimic a huge explosion.

The spectacle caught the attention of film director, Alan Parker, who negotiated with Waters to make the album's material into a movie. The decision was made not to script any dialogue and instead to use only the sections of music from the album. Bob Geldolf was given the lead role of Pink, though he originally baulked at the idea of working with an act that he saw as prog rock dinosaurs (his own music in Boomtown Rats moved between the raw attitude of punk and the wry stance of new wave). Prior to filming, Geldolf and his manager happened to get into a taxi that was being driven by Waters' brother-in-law and so Waters heard a firsthand account of how disinterested Geldolf was in the film.

Yet Geldolf warmed to the project and did an admirable job of inhabiting the character at its centre, while Waters himself ended up being the one who struggled with the project. After watching a rough cut, Waters insisted that the section of the film that featured 'Comfortably Numb' should be removed, since the accompanying footage was too bleak and made the film drag (though the fact that the embryo of the song had been written by Gilmour may have also played into his decision). Even with this edit in place, the film was filled with stark onscreen imagery that drew directly from the tortured personal narrative of Waters' songs and the result was melodramatic and humourless. Despite its failings, the film was a well-constructed piece, which flowed naturally from song to song and Scarfe's animations were skilfully blended into the main body of the movie. The result was a hallucinatory visual experience, which destined the film to become a cult classic.

Waters took full control of Pink Floyd for their next album, *The Final Cut* (1983), which was a vague meditation on the dreams of post-World War Two England. It was a fairly uneven effort and the other members of the group took solace in recording their own albums. Even Waters directed his attentions away from the band - releasing his first solo work, *The Pros and Cons of Hitchhiking* (1984).

It seemed as if Pink Floyd had come to an end and Waters was therefore stunned when he received news that Gilmour and Mason had decided to restart the group without him. He attempted to sue them for the use of the name, but after months of arguing they finally reached an agreement out of court. With Waters squeezed out of the band, it now made it possible for Wright to rejoin his two former colleagues. He returned just in time to take part in a massively successful world tour that followed the release of their album, *Momentary Lapse of Reason* (1987).

Waters was now free to explore his own ideas to their limit and he poured his energy into *Radio KAOS* (1987). It followed the struggles of a fictitious radio DJ working at a station that was changing its format in response to market research. The DJ was fighting for his right to choose what songs he would play and he was supported by a regular phone-in listener named 'Billy.' Waters brought in a retired DJ, Jim Ladd, to add an authentic voice to the album. Ladd's previous employer, KMET, had closed down after making a failed switch from rock to disco, much to the horror of its staff. The storyline seemed like it would offer a perfect opportunity for a set of rebellious, upbeat songs about defending creativity in music programming, but Waters taste for deep, personal tales made the recording seem claustrophobic. Billy was portrayed as a shut-in loner and the DJ's career came across as a lost cause.

Meanwhile, Waters' former bandmates slowly turned Pink Floyd into a more standard mid-tempo rock group, albeit one that could put on a live show that was both sonically and visually stunning. Waters had his own chance to relive the glory days of the group when he restaged *The Wall* as a concert in 1990 to celebrate the fall of the Berlin Wall. The show was held within the former no-man's land between East and West Berlin and the proceeds went to the Memorial Fund for Disaster Relief (the performers included Joni Mitchell, Van Morrison, Cyndi Lauper, Bryan Adams, The Scorpions, and Sinéad O'Connor).

Waters then went on to record *Amused to Death* (1992), which took its loose theme from Neil Postman's book, *Amusing Ourselves to Death*. The book attacked the media for failing to provide an indepth analysis of world events, leaving the viewers entertained rather than informed. The album received a strong critical reception, though Waters had already decided to take a hiatus from touring, so his career slowly faded throughout the nineties. He finally returned to the stage just before the turn of the new millennium, playing his greatest hits before sizable audiences.

Waters later rejoined the original Pink Floyd for a performance at *Live 8*, an event put on by Geldof to protest against Third World debt. This seemed to reinvigorate Waters' interest in touring and he spent the next two years performing songs from *Dark Side of the Moon* and then, in 2010, undertook a similarly intensive tour playing the entirety of *The Wall* (which led to a live film of one of these concerts being released in 2015). The songwriting ability of Waters and Pink Floyd may have long since faded, but it was clear that the legacy of their two greatest concept albums would continue long into the future.

Alan Parsons Project

The Alan Parsons Project were a group that emerged out of the wings of Pink Floyd. Parsons himself had been the engineer for *Dark Side of the Moon* and this led to him receiving a Grammy nomination. This experience gave him the confidence to start his own project, combining a laidback rock feel with his interest in studio experimentation. Yet, it is hard to think of a band as successful as the Alan Parsons Project who have been so often overlooked by history, especially since this wasn't a fly-by-night pop group, but an outfit with serious intent. Perhaps, in the end, their sound was too smooth and tautly produced for its own good.

Parson's own career had started in earnest after he heard *Sgt Pepper's Lonely Hearts Club Band* as a young sound engineer. He focused all his efforts on trying to get work at their regular

Roger Waters performing *The Wall* in concert in 2014. A film based on one of these concerts was released the following year. *(Garry Brandon)*

studio, Abbey Road, and his persistence paid off with him being employed as an assistant engineer for their next two albums (*Abbey Road* and *Let It Be*). While working at Abbey Road, Parsons met the session pianist, Eric Woolfson, who was already a successful songwriter (having written for Marianne Faithfull and Peter Noone from Herman's Hermits). They decided to work together and Woolfson also began to act as Parsons' manager, helping him to become one of the most in-demand producers working in the UK.

During the two years following the release of *Dark Side of the Moon*, the pair gathered together material for the first Alan Parsons Project album, *Tales of Mystery and Imagination* (1976), which was based on the short stories of Edgar Allan Poe. Parsons' studio experience meant that the music sounded state-of-the-art, layering lush synthesiser lines over slickly produced rock accompaniment and even incorporating one of the first uses of a vocoder (most strikingly on his version of "The Raven"). A number of professional musicians performed on the album and rather than just relying on Woolfson's vocals, the album also featured the singing of Terry Sylvester (The Hollies) and solo artist, John Miles (not to mention having Orson Welles narrating a couple of tracks).

Tales of Mystery and Imagination broke into the top forty-album chart in the US and began the trend of the band being more successful overseas than they were in their home country. However, there was some confusion about the band's line-up since they didn't ever perform live and, the following year,

Parsons was listed as the 'thirteenth best male vocalist of the year' in the industry magazine, *Cash Box* (despite the fact that he never sang on any of the group's albums).

The band took a similar approach to their next album, *I Robot* (1977), this time drawing inspiration from a short story collection by Isaac Asimov (though the comma was removed from the title since a TV company already owned the rights). This was a far more coherent effort – both in terms of the sound of the band and when considered as a conceptual piece.

Parsons wasn't scared of injecting a bit of pomp and drama into his music by using heavy layers of orchestration. However, on *I Robot*, he brought in fewer musicians and focused on using studio effects to create a very modern band sound – synths playing programmed arpeggios, bluesy guitars, and upfront pulsing bass lines. In this way, the early music of The Alan Parsons Project found a mid-point between the work of Rick Wakeman and Pink Floyd, which gained them a huge audience.

The songs on *I Robot* addressed the dangers of artificial intelligence – as the cover text noted: "[the human race's] brief dominance of this planet will probably end, because man tried to create robot in his own image." Though Parsons was careful to keep the lyrics loose enough that some of them could be released as singles and stand up in their own right. This was certainly the case with the breakthrough single off the album, 'I Wouldn't Want to be Like You," which Woolfson thought was from the perspective of a machine talking to a man, while Parsons thought it was the other way around!

I Robot (1977) by The Alan Parsons Project had a strongly articulated concept but still had singles that could stand alone. *(Hypgnosis)*

From this point onward, each of the Alan Parsons Project albums was based on a central theme: *Pyramid* (1978) was inspired by the Pyramids of Giza; *Eve* (1979) was about relations between men and women; and, *Turn of a Friendly Card* (1980) was about gambling.

As time went on, the central concepts at hand became more convoluted and hard to decipher. *Eye in the Sky* (1982) also seemed to take inspiration from Egyptian mythology and went on to be their best-selling album. It's most well-known song, 'Sirius', is still widely recognised today as the intro music that the Chicago Bulls play when they come out onto court.

The Alan Parsons Project had planned to release a double-album after this, which would look at the general public's relationship with modern technology. Instead, the most thematic tracks were collected on a single album, *Ammonia Avenue* (1984), while the leftovers were released as *Vulture Culture* (1985). The band's interest in popular culture continued on their next album, *Stereotomy* (1985), which looked at the failings of celebrity culture. Its title was taken from a phrase by Edgar Allan Poe that means to cut shapes from objects, though in this case it referred to the way fame shapes a successful person.

This run of high-concept pieces came to an end with *Gaudi* (1987), which was based on the life of Catalan architect, Antoni Gaudi (and was later made into a musical in Germany in 1993). The band's music no longer sounded as cutting edge as it had in the mid-seventies and they now blended in with the many soft rock groups of the era, causing them to be largely forgotten over the decades that followed.

Parsons did continue making music, going on to release a number of solo albums some of which were based around conceptual ideas - in particular *On Air* (1996) which is about man's discovery of flight and *The Time Machine* (1999) which is about the passage of time in one person's life.

The Time Machine is one of Alan Parsons' more solid solo efforts and shows his continued desire to release concept albums. *(Storm Studios)*

Yet, from the start of his solo career in the late eighties, Parsons could see that his conceptual approach was falling out of vogue: 'Unfortunately, "concept" has become a dirty word. I still do concept albums but I don't stress the point. I say forget the theme, so long as you enjoy the music.'

Woolfson escaped this dilemma by moving more distinctly into musical theatre - creating one work based on Poe's short stories (in 2003) and a musical, *The Gambler* (1997) - before he finally passed away on 2nd December 2009.

Rick Wakeman

Rick Wakeman's career was buoyed in the eighties by the growing popularity of his main instrument, the synthesiser. Nonetheless, Wakeman did go through another rough patch after leaving Yes (for a second time). He'd decided to take a long tax holiday in Switzerland, but this ended up ruining his marriage and eventually saw him marry the secretary from the recording studio where he was working. He was drinking heavily, without the focus to get another project off the ground.

Meanwhile, Yes had cast off their prog origins and morphed into an eighties pop group under the reins of remaining original member, Chris Squire. This must've put salt in the wound for Wakeman, though his career was finally saved when he was picked up by a huge management agency called M.A.M. They helped him sign a new deal with Charisma Records and, with their encouragement, Wakeman set about writing an album based on George Orwell's novel, *1984* (as Bowie had previously hoped to do).

Wakeman worked with Tim Rice - a lyricist who regularly worked with Andrew Lloyd Webber - as well bringing on board a number of well-known singers, including: Chaka Khan, Jon Anderson, and Steve Harley. The album was released near the end of 1980, reaching number 22 on the charts, and there were plans for a musical, but these were stifled by lawyers acting for Orwell's estate. For the most part, Wakeman abandoned the idea of doing themed work from this point onward, though he continued to release albums on a regular basis right through into the new millennium.

The Residents

The Residents emerged out of San Francisco and were one of the most prog-y groups never to be labelled as 'prog.' Their music was just as egg-headed, but its deep interest in the history of pop music gave it a core of melody and hookiness. Where prog tended to rely on flashy musicianship, the Residents' music was constructed from odd collages of sound that they came up with in the studio. This led them to be called 'post-punk' though their first single came out in 1972 when punk was still in its infancy so perhaps calling them 'experimental avant-pop' might be more appropriate (even if a little long-winded).

Their music needed to turn heads, since the band themselves remained anonymous throughout their career, relying instead on peculiar ad campaigns and carefully orchestrated interviews with representatives from their record company, The Cryptic Corporation (though many speculated that these record reps were the band members themselves).

Their early albums – *Meet the Residents* (1974) and *The Third Reich'n'Roll* (1976) – were constructed from samples and re-recorded snippets of early pop songs. The band's warped sensibility turned these cheesy hits into a creepy swamp of fascistically catchy hooks and seemed to expose an evil undercurrent that existed beneath modern pop music.

Further on in their career, things became even more peculiar with the release of *Eskimo* (1979), which purported to be the music of the indigenous peoples of the title, but instead goes from tribal chants into snippets from advertising and pop music. All of this weirdness was hardly the kind of thing that could get played on radio, so the band recorded a whole album of one minute songs (*The Commercial Album*, 1980) and then bought advertising space on a top forty radio station (KFRC), thereby forcing the station to play their music.

The band's clearest concept albums were their trio of albums about the battles between the Moles and the Chubs - *The Mark of the Mole* (1981), *The Tunes of Two Cities* (1982), and *The Big Bubble* (1985). Disturbingly, this series was initially planned to encompass six albums, though thankfully this was not completed.

During the seventies, the group had played live very seldom – disguising their identity by dressing as mummies or by wearing black cloaks or huge eyeball masks. However, the new multi-media possibilities that opened up in the eighties were too good to pass up and the band began to fuse their album concepts more coherently into their live shows. The group's *Cube E* set of performances (in 1989) encapsulated their interests, providing a history of modern American popular music by covering first the birth of country music, then the music of the African American slaves. Rather than trying to provide a serious historical narrative, the piece bluntly exposes the birth of rock music within America's race troubles. The third act introduces an Elvis character who steals aspects of each, before being 'killed' by the British Invasion. This last section draws from their album, *The King and Eye* (1989), while the whole work as a whole was finally released as *Cube E: Live in Holland (The History of American Music in 3 EZ Pieces)* (1990). Equally conceptual was their release, *God In Three Persons* (1990) about a pair of Siamese twins and their manager, who finally falls in love with one of them and severs them apart.

The Residents pushed the technological aspect of their work throughout their career, releasing one of the first music-related CD-ROMs in the early nineties. They eventually amassed over a hundred releases, though their cultural relevance steadily waned, especially when creating cut-up, collaged covers of classic works became a genre unto itself in the new millennium. Whether the Residents are considered a 'prog' group or not, they ended up suffering the same fate – their increasingly inscrutable work was abandoned by all but the most dedicated fans and they eventually came to seem like hold-outs from a former era.

The Legacy of Prog

The continued success of Pink Floyd and the Alan Parsons Project in the eighties made it seem as if prog might be ready for a return. These bands were joined by hard rockers, Styx, who also moved in a conceptual direction with the release of *Paradise Theater* (1981) which used a story about the decline of a classic movie theatre as a metaphor for Reagan's America. The band created a more concrete narrative on *Kilroy Was Here* (1983), describing a future in which rock'n'roll was banned (making it reminiscent of both *2112* by Rush and Pete Townshend's *Lifehouse* project). They then attempted to turn this into a live spectacle, with video sequences and large stage-sets, but the pressure of touring such a complex show re-ignited already existing tensions within the group and helped lead to their break-up.

The popular adoption of the synthesiser in the eighties didn't just help Rick Wakeman's career, it also provided a window for a neo-prog movement to emerge. Most notable of the newer acts to pick up on this opportunity was Marillion, who had stacked keyboard banks to rival Wakeman's and also incorporated layered guitar effects (a la U2) to produce slick hard rock tunes.

Their strongest conceptual effort was *Misplaced Childhood* (1985), which looked at how bad experiences with love in childhood can lead to struggles holding relationships together as an adult. Marillion made little impact on the charts from this point onward, but retained a reasonable fanbase of dedicated fans. Without the need to write commercial hits, Marillion made another attempt at a concept album on *Brave* (1994). At the time, the band was fronted by Steve Hogarth and the band's website features his description of how the lyrics for the album were inspired by a radio news report: 'The police had picked up a young woman wandering on the Severn Bridge who refused or was unable to speak to them. In desperation the appeal was broadcast to the general public in an attempt to discover her identity ... I thought we might dream up a story which would become a piece of music like a fictional documentary of her life and the circumstances which led her to the bridge. We now had a concept album on our hands at a time when the whole genre was, and probably still is, terribly unfashionable.'

This rebirth of prog was short-lived and musicians with prog leanings tended toward heavier music instead, kicking off a separate prog-metal movement (see Chapter Five). In fact, the continued association between prog and concept albums over this period may have been part of the reason that the form was not pursued by acts from outside this genre – it was seen as an artform in decline. Though in popular music, every good idea comes around again, so a couple of decades later some of the main aspects of prog would rear their head again, as we shall see in the final chapter of this book.

Chapter Five

The Metal Years

Metal bands have always made use of fantasy and horror imagery, splaying otherworldly images across their t-shirts, cover art, and tour posters. Some have also taken the next step and turned these into concept albums – so many in fact, that it's hard to cover the whole gamut. Many of the biggest names in metal have attempted concept albums, including Alice Cooper, Kiss, and Iron Maiden, and the subgenre of 'prog-metal' has alone been responsible for a raft of themed works. It was metal bands that kept the form alive during the eighties and early nineties, when it had fallen out of favour and it was also a metal artist, Marilyn Manson, that brought the form back to the attention of the wider public at the turn of the new millennium.

It is commonly acknowledged that heavy metal started with British group, Black Sabbath, who ushered in the genre's focus on the macabre with lyrics full of witches and black magic. However, it was a band from the other side of the Atlantic that would produce metal's first concept album. Singer, Vincent Furnier, already had a predilection for musical theatrics and horror-movie-inspired lyrics so it only took a bit of imagination to turn his dark inspirations into a storyline for his band, Alice Cooper...

Classic Metal

Alice Cooper made their reputation by introducing phantasmagorical elements to their performances, using props and costumes to create horror set pieces for each song. Furnier claimed he had been informed via ouija board that he was the reincarnation of a witch called 'Alice Cooper' so he took this for the name of his band. When the group started out in 1968, Alice Cooper's music was essentially classic rock, but by incorporating aspects of horror movies into their lyrics they followed the development of hard rock into heavy metal. Eventually, Furnier separated from the rest of his original bandmates and effectively became a solo act, though under the same name.

Some have taken Cooper's first album as a solo act, *Welcome To My Nightmare* (1975), to be a concept album though only the last few tracks hint that this might be the case – a song called 'Steven' introduces the main character and the previous tracks are supposedly his nightmares, though the album ends with his 'Awakening' and 'Escape.' The horror movie aspect was ratcheted up by having small sections of narration supplied by Vincent Price. While this didn't cohere together as a singular piece on record, it did inspire Cooper to have specific stage sets to be made that brought to life each of Steven's nightmares.

It wasn't until a few albums later that Alice Cooper's truly showed his ability to bring a theme to life across an album, but this time he drew from a terrible experience from his own life rather than fictional horror. *From The Inside* (1978) was inspired by Furnier's time in a mental asylum, where he was attempting

Alice Cooper cast aside his usual shock rock persona to sing about his experiences within a sanatorium on *From The Inside*. (Garry Brandon)

to recover from his alcohol abuse problems. Alice Cooper's playful depiction of life within a mental health ward helps the album move beyond the autobiographical (for example, the track 'Nurse Rozetta' about a patient developing a crush on a tough-minded hospital staff member).

The songs on *From The Inside* were written in collaboration with Bernie and manage to make a more general statement about the arc of drug abuse, from self-aggrandisement to self-destructive. This album started a trend of metal bands turning their experiences of hard living into conceptual works and Cooper's gruesome live shows provided an immense inspiration for later acts, especially Marilyn Manson (see below).

Cooper's interest in concept albums continued across his career, with the character of Steven making repeated appearances (most notably on the sequel, *Welcome 2 My Nightmare*, 2011) and another album that followed the story of a serial killer called 'Spider' (*Along Came A Spider*, 2008). Though it was his work from the seventies that continued to define him in the eyes of most fans.

Alice Cooper's immediate inheritors, in terms of onstage showmanship, were the flashy four-piece, Kiss, whose live shows were packed with pyrotechnics and gigantic stage sets. Each member wore black-and-white make-up that reflected their own fictional alter-egos – Paul Stanley (guitar/vocals) was The Starchild, Gene Simmons (bass/vocals) was The Demon, Ace Frehley (lead guitar/vocals) was Space Ace, and Pete Criss (drums/vocals) was The Catman. *Destroyer* (1976) created a loose storyline for each of their characters and helped inspire the Kiss comic that was published by Marvel Comics (the band's contribution was to arrange for their blood to be mixed with the red ink that was used for the first print run).

A ballad, 'Beth', off the album reached number seven in the US charts and the band were so emboldened by their success that they agreed to star in a TV movie, *Kiss Meet The Phantom of the Park*. The result was B-grade in the extreme – it is easy to spot Ace Frehley's black stunt-double replace him in some scenes and Peter Criss refused to turn up for post-production, so his voice was dubbed by a Hanna-Barbera cartoon actor.

These various creative projects set the band up well for attempting a concept album and they certainly had the ego for carrying through such a project – in 1978, the band had not only released a greatest hits compilation, but each member had also put out their own solo record in tandem. Yet their career was on a downward trajectory by the time they finally got around to attempting a narrative work – *(Music From) The Elder* (1981).

Their previous two albums had wavered between musical styles (even edging uncomfortably close to disco) and they lost many of their former fans, so it was an odd time to try such an ambitious project. The plot on *The Elder* revolves around a young man (known simply as 'the boy'), who has been chosen by the Council of Elders to be trained as a warrior. He gains confidence through the teachings of the old master, Morpheus, but he eventually decides he must find his own path by escaping from the island where he is being held. The music strove for the high drama of The Who's *Tommy* or the operatic mini-epics of Queen, but instead it came out sounding bloated and meandering. Bizarrely, three of the tracks were co-written by Lou Reed and the album was co-produced by Bob Ezrin (who'd previously worked on *The Wall*), but neither of these contributions saved it from being an incoherent mess. The album achieved only mediocre sales and the group began to wither away (Criss had already quit the band prior to this and Frehley left soon afterward). Simmons had originally hoped this work might lead to a movie project, but this pipedream was soon abandoned. Twenty years later, an online campaign was started by a young filmmaker in order to relaunch the project, though most Kiss fans would probably be happier if the album remained buried.

Danish metal singer, King Diamond, took up from where Kiss left off, distinguishing himself with a remarkable ear-shattering, operatic singing style. His black-and-white make-up proved too close for comfort for Gene Simmons and a legal battle ensued after Simmons saw the sleeve of *The Dark Sides EP* (1988) and found the artist's photograph a little too reminiscent of his own visage.

However Diamond's creative vision was far darker than that of Kiss and his strongest foray into the concept album was *Abigail* (1987) which told a gothic tale of the couple, Jonathan La'Fey and Miriam Natias. They move into the La'Fey family mansion, despite being warned by seven horsemen not to do so.

A ghost of one of his ancestors encourages Jonathan to kill his wife, because she is about to become pregnant with the spirit of the evil witch, Abigail La'Fey (named after Anton LaVey, who founded the Church of Satan). Sure enough, his wife turns out to be pregnant, but he ignores the warnings and ends up being killed himself. His wife also dies in childbirth, leaving only Abigail. King Diamond went on to further success with *Them* (1988) and its sequel, *Conspiracy* (1989). His career went underground after this, though he continued to release albums full of gruesome violence, incest, zombies, and insanity for the next two decades.

Blue Öyster Cult were another long-lasting metal group, who released their first album in 1972 and gradually found themselves a large fanbase by mixing straight-forward rock riffs with elements of horror and fantasy. Throughout their career, their manager, Sandy Pearlman, had contributed lyrics to the group and he always hoped that they might produce an album based on an alternative history of the world that he had written. However, they initially only drew on this material on individual songs and it took until the early eighties for him to have his chance. The band had fallen into a creative rut and Pearlman was helping their recently-departed drummer, Albert Bouchard, on a solo album. However, given that he'd only been the drummer in Blue Öyster Cult and Pearlman wasn't even a musician, the pair found it difficult to convince their record label to back the project. Instead, Pearlman ended up arranging for the latest line-up of Blue Öyster Cult to release *Imaginos*

(1988), without Bouchard even being involved. The band added new tracks to the album and arranged for guest appearances by guitar-shredder Joe Satriani and Robby Krieger (the Doors).

The plot of the album was hard to follow without the liner notes, but was impressive in scope – not surprising since Pearlman had been working on it for such a long time! The story centred on the godlike beings worshipped in Mexico and Haiti prior to colonisation, which he portrayed as aliens from outer space called Les Invisibles ('seven sleepers, seven sages, seven ladders to the seventh heaven'). These beings secretly controlled parts of world history and were responsible for the birth of a special child called 'Imaginos' in the US state of New Hampshire. As a young man, Imaginos travels the world and is eventually shipwrecked in Mexico, washing up on 'oyster beds plush as down' and it is here that he receives his first messages from Les Invisibles, drawing him into their cult (thus giving rise to the name, Blue Öyster Cult). He ends up being used as a puppet by the extraterrestrials in order to change the course of world events. As an old man, he finds himself drawn to an ancient Mayan temple in Mexico and discovers the 'Magna of Illusion,' which he gives to his daughter. She stores it in her attic, not realising that it is still emanating an evil influence on the world, sending thoughts into the minds of Europe's leaders, causing them to start World War I.

The fact that the songs themselves were reasonably opaque and were only faintly filled out by the sleeve notes, left fans searching out interviews with Pearlman to get a more complete picture. This helped add an air of mystery to the project, especially when it became clear that this would be the last window into the world of Les Invisibles. The conceptual aspect of Blue Öyster Cult was largely forgotten as they turned into a touring relic over the decades that followed, though their broad impact saw their music being covered by artists as diverse as Metallica, Wilco, and the Smashing Pumpkins.

The same year that *Imaginos* was released, England's most popular metal group, Iron Maiden, attempted their own concept album. Throughout their career the band's music had often drawn from literary sources, with songs based on the short stories of Edgar Allan Poe, Frank Herbert, and Samuel Taylor. They also had tracks that took inspiration from historical events such as the Native American struggle in the American West, the rise of Ancient Egypt, the conquests of Alexander the Great, and the prophecies of the Book of Revelations. Their live shows picked up on these themes by including entire set changes between songs and their distinctive album artwork incorporated the band's own mascot - a ragtag zombie called Eddie, who was placed in various guises depending on whether the group felt like drawing from fantasy, science fiction, or ancient history.

During the mid-eighties, the band's lead singer, Bruce Dickinson, began pushing for them to attempt a concept album. The other main songwriter within the group was guitar player, Steve Harris, and he wasn't so sure about the idea. Yet, in the lead-up to their seventh album, Harris finally found a concept that seemed perfect for them: 'I didn't really have a title for it or any ideas at all. Then I read the story of the seventh son, this mythical figure that was supposed to have all these paranormal gifts, like second sight and what have you, and it was more, at first, that it was just a good title for the seventh album, you know? But then I rang Bruce and started talking about it and the idea grew.'

Seventh Son of a Seventh Son (1988) had a number of tracks that were based around the paranormal, including 'The Prophecy,' 'The Clairvoyant,' and the title track itself. Many of the lyrics also reflected how the 'seventh son' was torn between using his powers to help the world and using them for profit. However, Dickinson later admitted to *Kerrang Legends* that the work was only loosely themed: 'It was only half a concept album. There was no attempt to see it all the way through, like we really should have done. *Seventh Son* has no story. It's about good and evil, heaven and hell, but isn't every Iron Maiden record?'

Seventh Son was hugely successful in the UK, with four songs hitting the top ten and the album taking the top spot on the charts. It was a popular time for concept albums by heavy metal artists and this was probably a reflection of the fact that metal itself had reached the zenith of its popularity. Concept albums became a way for new bands to differentiate themselves from the pack and some artists matched this conceptual depth with more complex musical approaches, leading some to claim that a new form of prog had now arrived on the scene ...

Prog Metal

The success of heavy metal throughout the eighties gave new acts the license to try fresh approaches to their music. The most ambitious of these acts begun to be referred to as 'prog metal,' though the groups varied widely – some were given this label because of their technical proficiency, while others were musically simplistic but had strong storytelling skills.

Queensrÿche seemed miles away from the prog rock moniker when they first started out. They were an American group that sounded like Iron Maiden, but their early look leant more towards glam sci-fi – jumpsuits, make-up, motorcycle gloves, and shiny jackets with overlarge clasps. They had a leaning toward the theatrical from the start due to their lead singer, Geoff Tate, who had studied opera and hence had formidable vocal range in the upper register, somewhere between a tenor vibrato and a blood-curdling scream. Their over-the-top fashion style eased as the 80s progressed and the band instead twisted their theatrical notions into their music.

Operation: Mindcrime (1988) had one of the most well-constructed narratives amongst the prog rock conceptual works. It told the story of a drug-addict called Nikki, who harbours a growing anger at the US political system and the secret wars it is funding in South America. He joins an underground movement, but ends up being brainwashed to become a mindless assassin who is controlled by the trigger-word 'mindcrime.' He seeks absolution from a prostitute-turned-nun

(Mary) and soon falls in love with her. However, when the mastermind of his crimes, Dr. X, finds out that Mary knows the truth about the killings, he tries to get Nikki to kill his beloved. In a daze, Nikki hurries to find Mary so that they can escape together, but when he arrives at the church he finds that she is already dead. Has he killed her or was it Dr. X? The listener is never quite sure, but trauma of the event is enough to drive Nikki insane and the album ends with him in a psych ward recalling what has happened.

The style of the music on *Operation: Mindcrime* might be too much characteristic of its time to allow it to become a classic concept album, but there are still many things to admire about the work as a whole. It was a good decision by the band to write a number of the songs focused on the themes of the album (politics, drug addiction, love), without tying them down to heavily to the plot. This allowed these songs to successfully stand on their own as singles, while they were contextualised on the album by having short sections of dialogue between the tracks (read by actors playing the parts of Dr. X and Mary). The musical scope of the album was also improved by the work done on it by well-known soundtrack composer Michael Kamen, who created orchestral parts that included a lush bed of instrumentation on the album's centrepiece, 'Suite Sister Mary' (which stretches out to 11 minutes and features a full Latin choir).

Operation: Mindcrime only achieved moderate sales at first, though it did sell well in the UK and Europe, where the notion of a hard rock band doing a concept album was considered less unusual. However, the album did eventually reach gold in the US, helped by the release of nine music videos and a rise in profile that came after Queensrÿche supported Metallica for a national tour. Their next album, *Empire* (1990), was an even greater commercial success, but Queensrÿche were still excited about the *Operation: Mindcrime* project and used their growing budget for live shows to create a show-within-a-show section of their performance, where they played the main songs from the album against a set of video backdrops that detailed the storyline. Over the years that followed, there was talk of making *Operation: Mindcrime* into a movie and Tate even employed a screenwriter to work on it. The band were also approached by the Tony-Award-nominated theatre actor, Adam Pascal, about turning it into a stage play.

Meanwhile, the audience for the band's music was beginning to dwindle and they lacked the finances to carry through either of these plans to completion. The band did attempt a follow-up album, *Operation: Mindcrime II* (2006), but it ended up being a weak postscript for an idea whose time had already past.

Savatage came out of a similar era of US heavy metal, though they were closer to classic heavy metal and were often tied into the so called 'hair metal' scene that was popular at this time. Like Queensrÿche, they were labelled as 'prog metal' more for their conceptual, theatrical approach than their musical style. The band were headed by two brothers, Jon and Criss Oliva. Their first move towards conceptual material was on *Gutter*

Ballet (1989), which had a trio of songs ('Mentally Yours', 'Summer's Rain', 'Thorazine Shuffle') that featured the same character struggling with mental illness. The music also moved in a more theatrical, progressive direction after Jon was enraptured by a live performance of *Phantom of the Opera*. This aspect of their music was helped along by producer and songwriting collaborator, Paul O'Neill, who had played guitar for touring versions of the musicals, *Hair* and *Jesus Christ Superstar*.

Savatage's most accomplished conceptual piece was *Streets: A Rock Opera* (1991), which saw the band leaning heavily on power ballads and heightening their sound with strings and, at one point, a children's choir. The storyline in the liner notes is based on a novel by O'Neill and tells the story of rock star, DT Jesus, who spends his early life as a drug dealer, before switching to music. His career takes off, but he is stopped in his tracks when his best friend is stabbed by an enemy from his drug dealing days. This sends him into a downward spiral that eventually sees him back out on the streets.

The band's progress was dealt a tragic blow in 1993, when Criss was killed by a drunk driver. Jon eventually decided to keep making music under the name, Savatage, and they released a number of other themed albums over the years that followed, with O'Neill continuing to write lyrics and liner notes/poems when required. *Dead Winter Dead* (1995) was one of the more coherent efforts and was based around the conflict in Sarajevo during the early nineties. The thought process behind *The Wake Of Magellan* (1997) was less clear in its attempt to blend together a number of disparate stories into one narrative. The band made a new start on *Poets And Madmen* (2001) and Jon Oliva took over lead vocals, after years of taking a back-seat. The storyline begins with a journalist being placed in a mental asylum after years of covering famines in Africa, but his past is eventually uncovered by three teenagers who break into the institution. Yet there would be no great reawakening for Savatage, whose musical style was too far out of line for contemporary tastes and even their name was a throwback to a now extinct period of musical history.

At the opposite end of the metal spectrum from Queensrÿche and Savatage were the proponents of industrial metal. Some of these groups were also labelled as prog, but not for their symphonic influences, but rather the intricate approach they took to their music.

Canadian group, Voivod, were at the industrial end of prog metal and had a rhythm section that were almost machine-like in their ability to switch between complex rhythm patterns and time signatures. Their lyrics repeatedly made reference to a futuristic world that is inhabited by a character called Voivod. The title of their album, *Dimension Hatross* (1988), apparently referred to a new universe that Voivod created by causing light-speed collisions between protons and anti-protons. The genre of industrial metal also spawned Fear Factory, who shared Voivod's interest in sci-fi lyricism. Their early work often returned to the theme of technology being in conflict with the

CONCEPT ALBUMS

human race that created it. This concept came to fruition on *Obsolete* (2001), which presented a Terminator-like future, in which a hero called Edgecrusher battled against the machines that were attempting to take control of society.

Dream Theatre were the most natural inheritors of the 'prog metal' label since all the group's members were technically brilliant musicians that wanted to push beyond the usual structures of popular music. The original line-up were all attending Berklee School of Music when they met in Boston in 1987. They had chops to burn and wanted to take out their talents on something a little more complicated than your standard heavy metal. By the time they came to record a concept album, they had added a keyboard player and were mixing their hard rocking guitar-work with ominous synthesised sounds. *Metropolis Part 2: Scenes From A Memory* (1999) was a sequel to a track on an earlier album, which described a man who is having flashbacks of the murder of a woman in 1928. He finds himself haunted by the killing and is driven to solve the crime. Like classic prog albums, many of the tracks are long and involve multiple movements, creating a work that has a symphonic feel.

From these examples, it's clear that a broad range of work has been labelled 'prog metal' and often it is the conceptual aspirations of the artists rather than their musical style which leads them to be categorised under this name. Many of these bands would've been too extreme for a popular audience, even in the heyday of metal during the eighties. This situation became even worse during the following decade, leaving many metal artists forced to choose between taking a more accessible approach or retreating into ever more subdivided subgenres.

Surviving the Nineties

The arrival of grunge in the early nineties seemed to signal another cultural shift away from the concept album. Any music that wreaked of pretentiousness was an anathema to grunge, just as it had been to the punk scene in the late seventies. Literary influences did creep into the lyrics of Kurt Cobain, but they were channelled into abrupt aphorisms that were delivered in a mumble. It was clear that you couldn't have the laidback attitude of a slacker and still have the energy to produce epic album structures. The metal acts that remained in the mainstream were the ones that adjusted most successively to these new trends – even a juggernaut like Metallica were driven to cut their hair short and begin writing punchy, short numbers.

The heavy metal acts that continued to produce concept albums tended to be either older acts that had decided to continue on regardless or new artists who'd emerged from the ever more extreme sub-genres that were now being created in the metal underground.

W.A.S.P. seemed like one of the least likely metal groups to survive the transition into the nineties, since they were pure L.A. glam rock. They had more make-up than Twisted Sister and more onstage gimmicks than Alice Cooper. A typical show saw the half-naked nuns being tortured and the mock-slaughter of live pigs that ended with pre-prepared chunks of meat being thrown into the audience. Yet the lead singer, Blackie Lawless, had already survived a tour filling in as a guitarist for drug-addled punks, The New York Dolls, and was undeterred by having a flaming codpiece explode during one early W.A.S.P show, so he wasn't going to quit now.

The ongoing functioning of W.A.S.P. as a musical unit relied upon finally getting rid of guitar player, Chris Holmes, whose relentless alcohol binges were made infamous by an appearance in the documentary, *The Decline of Western Civilisation Part II: The Metal Years*. Lawless then released a surprisingly coherent concept album, *The Crimson Idol* (1992), which detailed the rise and fall of a recalcitrant rock star (a topic Lawless was in a good position to write about). The interest generated from this album meant that the band were able to retain a moderate following in the US, even while many of their counterparts in the glam scene sunk without a trace. They were still going a decade later and again made an attempt at metal storytelling on two successive albums: *The Neon God Part One: The Rise* (2004) and *Part Two: The Demise* (2004). These works were creative failures, which directly appropriated ideas from The Who's *Tommy* - Part One begins with an overture just as *Tommy* had done, it includes a libretto on the sleeve, and features a main character (a telepathic orphan) who ends up starting his own cult.

The musical career of Ronnie James Dio went even further back than that of Blackie Lawless, though he remained firmly devoted to traditional metal – initially singing for Rainbow and Black Sabbath, before becoming a successful solo artist (playing simply as 'Dio'). His music had always been wedded to medieval imagery through its artwork and lyrics and *Magica* (2000) brought all this together into a single work of fantastical mythology. On an eighteen minute track at the end of the album, Dio read out the full back-story which the songs had been based upon. 'Magica' is a book of spells that is taken by the evil character, Shadowcast, when his evil army take control of the city of 'Blessing.' An old wizard called Eriel remains free and manages to sneak close enough to the book of Magica to memorise a 'restoration' spell before he is captured, but the spell needs three days to recite. He manages to pass on the spell to a young man (Challis), before he is killed. Challis is able to cast the spell which restores his people to their rightful place and it is revealed that he is actually Eriel's son.

The narrative had many elements of a classic 'fairytale', but the inclusion of crucifixion scenes, not to mention the spiritual rapture that ensues when the restoration spell is cast, gave the secularly titled 'Magica' a decidedly religious flavour. Dio's plan for follow-up albums based on this same world never eventuated, though he did continue recording music and touring right up until his death in 2010.

It was fortunate for Dio and W.A.S.P. that they had a legacy which they could draw upon to survive the nineties, but things were much harder for newer metal groups that emerged over this time. Grunge had tamed the heavy guitars of metal and combined them with a more laidback style of clothing, which was also matched by lyrical content that was far more down-to-earth. More traditionalist metal groups responded by retrenching more firmly into the style of metal which they had adopted and this led to an explosion in sub-genres. Many of these were less conducive to allowing a storyline to be put across. For example, death metal proponents focused on producing compressed tracks of pure aggression, with the velocity of speed metal being pushed to new extremes and growling vocals that didn't allow much chance of a coherent storyline being put across.

Dramatic lyrical content was central within the theatrical style of black metal and hence it was a genre that was more amenable to producing concept albums. English group, Cradle of Filth, created gothic and symphonic metal pieces that were often inspired by real life mass murderers from history. *Cruelty and the Beast* (1998) was about the blood countess Elizabeth Bathory, who was accused of killing dozens (possibly hundreds) of young girls during the 1600s in Romania (rumours circulated that she wanted to bathe in virgin's blood to retain her youth). Similarly gruesome was *Godspeed on Devil's Thunder* (2008), which was inspired by Gilles de Rais, who lived as a nobleman in France during the 1400s. Despite purporting to be a devoted Christian, he in fact took part in late night rituals of murder, rape, and torture which eventually saw him hanged and his name stripped from all official records of the time.

Despite, the growing popularity of rhythm-heavy subgenres like death metal, black metal, and industrial metal, a new wave of metallers emerged who were focused on bringing back the melodic approach of the eighties. This new wave of power metal also took up the concept album as a way to assimilate the fantastical imagery of their metal forebears.

Iced Earth arrived just as grunge was beginning to take over the hard rock scene, but they stubbornly stuck with the power metal style they'd grown up with - gradually moving from Iron Maiden sound-a-likes to gain a style of their own. *Night Of The Stormbringer* (1992) told the story of a man who has lost his faith in god and become a harbinger of doom and destruction. Their career then went on hold for three years, with the band refusing to play or record again until their label re-wrote the unfair contract that they had originally signed. Their comeback in 1995 saw them release two albums in quick succession. The second was an album based on the comic series, *Spawn*, and its author Todd McFarlane even agreed to illustrate the album cover. This was the strongest and most well-known of the band's conceptual works, though they continued to release themed material over the decade that followed – most notably, *Horror Show* (2001) which was an ode to their favourite horror movies and *The Glorious Burden* (2004) which told the story of the US Civil War. Following a similar musical vein, Steel Prophet took inspiration from outside work, most notably on *Dark Hallucinations* (1999), which was based on Ray Bradbury's novel

Farenheit 451, and Blind Guardian from Germany released *Nightfall in Middle Earth* (1998) based on Tolkien's *Silmarillion*.

In the end, it seems that grunge didn't so much kill the concept album as drive it underground. It seemed that this trend would continue with the arrival of nu-metal in the late-nineties – a style which tried to inject heavy music with the rhythmic feel of hip hop and the in-your-face attitude of punk. The lyrics were drawn from real life rather than fantasy and the associated fashion was based in streetwear rather than trying to make a more extreme visual statement. Yet there was one artist who eschewed nu-metal, but nonetheless managed to break through from the metal underground and he used the concept album as a way to attack contemporary society and its basis in Christian morality...

Marilyn Manson

Marilyn Manson first exploded onto music television in 1995 with his sinister cover of 'Sweet Dreams' (by 80s pop group, The Eurythmics). His look brought the shock-rock imagery of Alice Cooper up to date by adding elements of bondage, punk, and B-grade horror. One might've expected that the band's sharp rise to fame would've been followed by an equally sharp decline, but in fact the group's aspirations went far beyond the gimmicky, shock tactics of their first single. Manson had a deeper vision he wanted to bring to the world and the heavy industrial sound of his early releases were given a grinding ferocity by producer, Trent Reznor, who also signed the band to his label, Nothing Records.

Reznor's own group, Nine Inch Nails (NIN), had done a great deal to popularise the sound of industrial metal and show that it could also be used to create more downbeat, moody tracks. NIN also released albums with a thematic base, most notably *Downward Spiral* (1994), which mapped a man's decline into madness. Many felt that this album had a strong influence on Manson's second album, *Antichrist Superstar* (1996), but this was a claim that Manson disputed in his autobiography: 'No matter what anyone said, I knew that *Antichrist Superstar* was not the same as *Downward Spiral*, which was about Trent's descent into an inner, solipsistic world of self-torment and wretchedness. *Antichrist Superstar* was about using your power, not your misery, and watching that power destroy you and everyone else around you.'

The title of *Antichrist Superstar* is a play on the title of Andrew Lloyd Webber's musical, *Jesus Christ Superstar*, making a mockery of the stage play's chirpy, lightweight narrative. Manson divided his album into three 'cycles' – 'The Heirophant,' 'Inauguration of the Worm,' and 'Disintegrator Rising.' These parts follow a loose progression that is based upon the stages of Manson's life, with his general disgust at society outlined in cycle one, before he introduces an alter-ego (Little Horn or Wormboy) to represent his early years in cycle two. In the final section, the protagonist grows in power and begins to see the rot at the heart of the culture around him. He realises that his fellow citizens are unworthy of being saved, so he instead decides that civilisation itself should be destroyed.

In fact, *Antichrist Superstar* was the first in a trio of Marilyn Manson albums that all revolved around a similar central theme – a main protagonist is shown achieving a level of success and/or notoriety, but this vantage point allows him to see the failures of society around him and eventually skews his viewpoint towards nihilism. To some degree, each album was a glorified autobiography of Manson himself, though they also presented a Nietzschean view of the world – with only a few clearheaded 'supermen' within a wider population that were sheeplike and kept docile by religion. Manson's own abusive treatment of groupies showed that he carried this disdain of others through to his offstage persona and his interest in decrying the morals of society saw him befriending the founder of the Church of Satan, Anton LaVey (who bestowed on Manson the title of Reverend). Despite this, Manson claimed he was not a Satanist and instead took the oppositional name of 'antichrist' to reflect his desire to free society from the teachings of Christianity.

Marilyn Manson's second album, *Mechanical Animals* (1998), channels his ideas through the viewpoint of a fictional character, 'Alpha.' On this occasion, Manson's aim is to critique celebrity culture and the narrative therefore derives an even influence from his own rise to fame. Other tracks on the album are supposedly sung by a rock star from outer space named 'Omega,' while the 'Mechanical Animals' of the album title are his band. The inspiration of Ziggy Stardust was clear, given that Manson's alien rock star was also an asexual being and went through a similar decline and fall. The album's artwork managed to take this one step further and the cover showed an impressively realistic image of a naked Marilyn Manson with a sculpted body that had six fingers and no genitalia aside from a pair of smoothed-over breasts. Inside the booklet, fans found that there was a second cover that related to the 'Omega' side of the album and also sections of text that were only readable once they were seen through the blue tint of the album's CD case.

The band's music morphed to match the subject matter, taking on a glam rock feel to fit with Omega's world of hedonism and drug use, though some Manson fans were disappointed that his music had lost its heavy industrial edge. *Mechanical Animals* raised the ire of Christian groups in the US, despite the fact that Manson's focus had moved from religion to celebrity. It probably didn't help that many of the successful singles off the album were the 'Omega' tracks which seemed to promote drug use and debauchery ('I Don't Like the Drugs, but the Drugs Like Me' and 'Dope Show'). Manson's music was blamed for providing inspiration to the teenage perpetrators of the school killings at Columbine High School, which resulted in seven deaths including the shooters themselves. Marilyn Manson refused to be interviewed over this period and instead focused his frustrations onto his next album *Holy Wood (In the Shadow of the Valley of Death)* (2000).

Holy Wood focused on the corporate media conglomerates and

Marilyn Manson took the shock approach of Alice Cooper to a new level and wrote three concept albums about religion, fame, and celebrity *(Garry Brandon)*

their connection to the world of the rich and famous. On this occasion, Manson takes Christian teachings as a framework to tell the story of 'Adam Kadmon' (named after the original man in the Jewish Kabbala). He lives in a world that is in the grasp of 'Celebritarianism,' which is a religion based around celebrities who have been immortalised by their violent deaths. The key figure is John F. Kennedy who takes the place of Christ in this new belief system, while the symbology of the crucifix is replaced by images of guns (this is shown literally on the cover, with a rifle and two handguns lain out to make a cross).

On this album, Manson's main thematic preoccupations found their clearest representation, even if the underlying storyline is just as hazy as his previous works. Rumours later surfaced that Manson had written an entire novel that was intended to go along with the album, though an apparent disagreement with his publishers meant it was never released. Manson also suggested that the run of three albums above could even be seen as a trilogy in reverse, with *Holy Wood* describing the rise of a young celebrity, who eventually becomes disillusioned with fame (on *Mechanical Animals*), but uses his success to gain control of society and eventually to destroy it (on *Antichrist Superstar*). Marilyn Manson gradually became less active after the completion of this trilogy and it is most likely this set of albums that he will be remembered for.

While it's true that the albums mentioned above only loosely fit the concept album mould, they nonetheless helped reinvigorate interest in the form and showed that conceptual work could still reach a broad popular audience. As his own creative power waned, he began to feel that his approach was being watered down by newer artists such as My Chemical Romance (see Chapter Seven). He even disparaged the group in one of his songs ('Mutilation is The Sincerest Form of Flattery') and bitterly told The London Paper: 'I'm embarrassed to be me because these people are doing a really sad, pitiful, shallow version of what I've done.'

In turn, Alice Cooper was equally unimpressed with how Manson had drawn from his own work and so it seems that no one in this line of acts was quite happy with the younger acts that they had inadvertently inspired!

The Legacy of the Metal Years

The adoption of the concept album within heavy metal had very little effect outside this genre (with the possible exception of Marilyn Manson's work). Even within metal, some sub-genres were moving away from conceptual work at the exact same time that others were moving towards it. These different currents meant that metal music was never tied so directly to the concept album as prog music had been and this stopped the form from being written off as 'something only metal artists do.'

Within the metal scene itself, the concept album was constantly reinvigorated by subsequent generations of musicians and this trend continues to the present day, as we shall see in the final chapter of this book.

Chapter Six

Hip Hop & Alternative Rock

The musical scene in the nineties may have seemed an anathema to concept albums, given the punk-influenced approach taken by grunge and the rise of commercially-minded nu-metal, as well as the continued success of straight-up rock acts like Guns'n'Roses. It looked as if writing longer form pieces would only be the preserve of underground metal groups (or perhaps electronica groups like The Orb, whose instrumental, tripped-out epics did claim to be about single topics).

However, as the turn of the millennium approached, things began to change. Concept albums may have remained too out-of-fashion for mainstream rock acts, but there were acts on the outskirts beginning to take steps in a conceptual direction. The punchy, streetwise approach of early hip hop was gradually expanded to allow more complex musical statements and this eventually led to fully-fledged concept albums by Prince Paul, Deltron 3030, and The Streets. Meanwhile, the so-called 'alternative rock' scene that had developed around grunge eventually became difficult to distinguish from the mainstream rock that it was attempting to dethrone. The newer acts that emerged on student radio stations began to take a different approach – producing more studied lyrics and slowly setting the stage for thematic work to be released.

Hip Hop

When rap first emerged on the New York music scene in the late 70s, it was used as a way for record spinning DJs to add a live element to the parties which they were putting on. Yet the form developed quickly and the subject matter of hip hop soon expanded to incorporate a storytelling aspect, though usually the lyrics gave snippets of the rapper's own biography rather than trying to tell a complete tale over a whole album. Rap groups often created strong imagery to go along with their work and this meant that some albums seemed larger than a sum of their individual tracks.

One example of this is Public Enemy, whose work was linked together by their focus on the struggle of African Americans. The group reflected their message of black unity by dressing in the fashion of the Black Panthers and intersecting their music with sections of speeches by figures such as Malcolm X and Martin Luther King. In an interview with Billboard magazine, lead rapper Chuck D explained how their third album, *Fear of a Black Planet* (1990), focused their political ideas around a specific philosophical vision: '[the album] was breaking down Dr. Frances Cress Wesling's colour confrontation theory about race and compressing it into the previously adolescent space of rap music and hip-hop. As a concept album, *Fear* challenged the purity of race by stating the world was a planet of colour that was not inferior to the Western status quo.'

Yet, the popularity of 'conscious' rap soon found itself taking a backseat to the sudden explosion of gangsta rap, with the arrival of *Straight Outta Compton* (1988) by N.W.A. It was at this point that rap's interest in the everyday experience of blacks in America began to focus more on gritty tales of lived experience, rather than trying to make a broader political statement. Stories of hustlers and drug dealers took centre stage in the lyrics of many rap acts and this narrowing of focus caused a reduction in the range of subject material that was represented. This was not usually enough to justify calling them concept albums, though the label might be applied to Jay-Z's work on *American Gangster* (2007), which took its inspiration from the film of the same name starring Denzel Washington.

De La Soul moved against the tide of gangsta rap. Their debut album, *3 Feet High and Rising* (1989), purposefully used bright colours and images of flowers to make them stand out from the legions of gangsta rap groups for whom such images would've been laughed out of the studio. Individual tracks on the album weren't connected, but were held together by skits and often drew from their own unique terminology – for example, the daisies shown on the cover were meant to be a representative acronym for the phrase 'DA Inner Sound Y'all.' However, De La Soul moved away from this approach soon afterward, frustrated with being misunderstood as a group of hip hop hippies.

The early De La Soul albums featured production work by Prince Paul, who had originally started his career in the group Stetsasonic. He later moved on to join gangsta rap group, Gravediggaz, but he kept his interest in pushing hip hop forward. He saw that the lyricism of rap meant it was the perfect medium for storytelling, especially since most hip hop tracks contained far more lyrics than your average rock song (due to the fact that rappers were not slowed down by keeping to a melody line and could hence deliver their lines at a furious speed). This eventually led him to record hip hop's most cohesive concept album, *Prince Among Thieves* (1999), which was heralded by respected music critic Robert Christgau as 'the closest thing to a true rock opera you've ever heard.'

One striking innovation that Prince Paul brought to the concept album was the extensive use of guest artists on the recording, which created a cast of characters more like a stage musical would have. This was possible for Prince Paul because he was acting as a composer and producer on the album, rather than needing to front the piece as a rock band. We might contrast this to *Tommy* by The Who, which was recorded entirely by members of the band themselves (with Townshend and Daltrey performing most of the vocals) and it was only when it was later made into a movie and then a musical that the parts were given to multiple singers.

The story of *Prince Among Thieves* revolves around a young rapper called Tariq (performed by Breezly Brewin), who is desperate to make enough money to record a demo tape. His friend, True (performed by Big Sha), convinces Tariq that he should work with him as a drug dealer until he has enough money. On the way, the pair meet a raft of characters who are each performed by luminaries from the hip hop fraternity – RZA plays a record label rep, Chris Rock and De La Soul appear as crack addicts, Everlast is a crooked cop, Big Daddy Kane plays the drug dealing kingpin, and Xzhibit appears as a prisoner. Eventually it turns out that True has only offered Tariq work as a drug dealer to get him out of the way, so True himself can steal the recording session and take the meeting with the record company exec. In a final showdown, Tariq shoots True and is taken away by the police.

There were plans for *Prince Among Thieves* to be made into a movie and a sharp-looking trailer was filmed for the project, featuring many of the high profile cast. However, despite strong reviews, album sales were very poor, and eventually the backing for a film dried up. Prince Paul was sorely disappointed and funnelled this frustration into his next album, *The Politics of the Business* (2003). Unsurprisingly, an entire album of bitterness about the music industry doesn't make for a very satisfying listen. The overall concept did have an element of humour – given its conceit of being a concept album about how to follow up an unsuccessful concept album - and the appearance of Dave Chappelle as a record exec is entertaining.

Yet overall it's a dreary listen. Prince Paul's career faltered after this point, though he continued to work on occasional musical projects and hosted his own radio show. *Prince Among Thieves* remains as the high water mark of his career and deserves to be remembered as one of the most ambitious works to have come out of hip hop.

Throughout the mid-period of Prince Paul's career he often collaborated with another groundbreaking hip hop producer, Dan The Automator (Dan Nakamura), and the pair released one of the most unusual hip hop albums of the nineties - *So...How's Your Girl?* (1999) - under the group name, Handsome Boy Modelling School. Once again skits were used to break up the music and, on this occasion, many of them were drawn from a single episode of the television show, *Get A Life*.

Dan The Automator delved even further into conceptual work on his next release, *Deltron 3030* (2000). For this project, he worked with rapper, Del the Funky Homosapien (Teren Delvon Jones) whose career had been kickstarted in 1991 by the breakthrough hit, 'Mistadobalina' (produced by Del's cousin, Ice Cube, from NWA). Del wasn't satisfied just being a one-hit wonder and had spent the intervening years pushing his craft into more challenging areas, making him the perfect frontman for Deltron 3030.

The album took up where the afro-futurism of Parliament had left off and created its own set of fictional characters, each played by a member of the group – Del became Deltron Zero and Dan The Automator called himself the Cantankerous

Captain Aptos, while the turntablist Kid Koala featured as Skiznod The Boy Wonder. The storyline was conceived over a couple of weeks and set Deltron Zero against an evil world empire that wants to eradicate hip hop because of its dangerous truth-telling ability. Del is a part-android soldier and computer genius, who uses his skill at rhyming to defeat each foe that his enemies send against him. This cosmic backstory and its cinematic, orchestral backing music meant that the album was limited to only a cult following, though it received great critical acclaim.

Fortunately for Dan the Automator, he'd already become involved in another project that would go on to be tremendously successful. He was asked by Damon Albarn (Blur) to join a new group, the Gorillaz, which would be represented to the public only as a set of cartoon characters. Albarn had featured on one of the Deltron 3030 tracks and Del the Funky Homosapien returned the favour by dropping a verse on the Gorillaz's breakthrough single, 'Clint Eastwood.' An important collaborator on the project was the comic artist, Jamie Hewlett, who produced all the group's art work and music videos. The songs themselves may not have been linked, but the band had cartoon alter-egos as striking as Ziggy Stardust or Alice Cooper which they used to project themselves to the world and this created a backbone of imagery for their work. Albarn and Hewlett had planned to eventually create a film using these same characters, but the creative partnership came to an end before this plan could be realised.

It was left to another UK-based group to take hip hop further into the world of concept albums. The Streets came out of the UK grime and garage rap scenes, which combined rap with the more established electronica and reggae traditions that existed in England. The Streets were one of the most successful acts to emerge from this milieu and their rise to fame was due in large part to the storytelling skills of the group's founder, Mike Skinner, who told true-to-life tales of the English working class.

On their second album, *A Grand Don't Come For Free* (2004), Skinner constructed a whole fictional storyline that kicked off with his protagonist losing a grand (£1000), while carrying out some everyday chores. He gambles to regain the money, though he fails to make it to the bookmakers in time to place his final bet (which turns out to be lucky, since he would've lost it all). Meanwhile, he has just started a new relationship with a woman named 'Simone,' but his fortunes in love go through similar vicissitudes. Just when the relationship seems to be getting serious, he sees her in a nightclub kissing one of his friends and after an attempt to win her back, the pair finally part.

The album concludes in an unusual manner by positing two possible endings, both of which start with his television breaking down. In the first, his bitterness leads him to get into a fight with the repairman; whilst in the second he finds the grand that he had originally lost in the back of his TV set. The success of *A Grand Don't Come For Free* is its ability to mix levity and emotional honesty to reflect the ups and downs of everyday

Damon Albarn (shown here in the Gorillaz) released loosely themed albums in Blur and later joined the cast on the breakthrough hip hop concept album, Deltron 3030. *(Garry Brandon)*

life. Rather than creating a concept album that strives to create an extraordinary mythology, he uses narrative to make his songs seem as if they are all drawn from a single person's life and, in this way, infuses them with a sense of realism.

A Grand Don't Come For Free showed that concept albums didn't need to be fantastical or surrealistic to grab the listener's interest. In this respect, his work was similar to some of the ultra-realist works that had come out of the English alternative rock scene over the preceding decade and we will turn to these next...

Alternative Rock

The rise of so-called 'alternative rock' in the nineties was primarily a widespread acceptance of the music that had been previously relegated to student radio stations. The rawness of punk had spread into other, less aggressive forms of music and this allowed for a more lo-fi aesthetic to become prevalent. Along with rejecting the slick recording techniques that had become so prevalent in the eighties, these artists also felt freer to move beyond the conventional love song into broader lyrical material.

As more of these artists gained popular success, the phrase 'alternative rock' came to have less meaning and was eventually abandoned. Even though these musicians eschewed complex musical structures (decrying them as pretentious, just as the punks had before them), the alternative rock scene nonetheless ended up paving the way for the re-emergence of concept albums in the new millennium. Many of the albums mentioned over the next few pages might be seen as particularly weak examples of a concept album, but it nonetheless seems worthwhile to notice how a number of the more adventurous and ground-breaking acts of this era still gravitated toward a conceptual approach.

This was especially the case in the UK, where the Brit-pop explosion, seeded by the success of the Stone Roses, was largely seen as a return to the classic British rock sounds of the sixties. This scene also produced Blur, who were fronted by Damon Albarn (already mentioned above for his work in the Gorillaz). Blur released a trio of albums that centred on modern life in England - *Modern Life is Rubbish* (1993), *Parklife* (1994), and *The Great Escape* (1995). 'Britishness' became a theme with which to connect their songs together into a coherent whole, in the same way it had been for the Kinks.

Parklife was the most cohesive effort of the three and Albarn later explained to NME that he saw it as "a loosely linked concept album involving all these different stories. It's the travels of the mystical lager-eater, seeing what's going on in the world and commenting on it."

Interestingly, the title track of *Parklife* featured the actor Phil Daniels from the *Quadrophenia* movie and one of the album cuts, 'Clover Over Dover,' has its protagonist considering throwing himself over the white cliffs which is reminiscent of Jimmy's own contemplation of suicide at the end of that movie. In this way, Blur made a direct connection between their interest in social commentary and the realist phase of the Who's work.

Radiohead emerged at the tail end of Brit-pop and initially their music was fairly standard alternative rock. The band came into their own on *OK Computer* (1997), which was filled with paranoiac visions of a disconnected, fragmented society. The sudden introduction of electronica blips and beats gave the sense that the individual tracks were all inspired by a new, coherent musical vision. What's more, the lyrics had an abstract feel to them as if they'd been pieced together from phrases about modern life and technology. These aspects made this album seem like it was portraying a larger vision, though on the documentary, *Meeting People Is Easy*, Thom Yorke, vented his frustration with journalists that called it a concept album: 'If they're gonna call it a concept album - if they're gonna fuck us on the technology angle - then let them. It's fucking noise anyway. We've done our job. We add to the noise, that's all.'

The group's drummer, Ed O'Brien, was more circumspect in an interview with the Guardian around the same time: 'We spent two weeks track-listing the album. The context of each song is really important... It's not a concept album but there is a continuity there.'

This rejection of the concept album tag reflects how negatively this form was viewed at this point in time. For many, it only conjured up resonances of pedantically complex musical structures, insanely expensive stage props, and didactic, overwrought lyrics. The thematic releases of Radiohead and

Blur didn't tick these boxes, so they weren't seen to fit to be labelled as concept albums, though this probably had more to do with the mood of the times (if they'd released this work in the seventies then the tag surely would've been applied).

In any case, both bands had clearly moved in a conceptual direction and this showed that there might again be room in popular music for albums that were held together by a central set of ideas. Certainly this was the opinion of David Bowie, who gradually re-adopted the concept album during the nineties, after a decade of releasing more standard pop and rock records.

It may seem odd to include David Bowie within a section of much younger acts but, as with all of Bowie's boldest moves, through the nineties he made a purposeful pivot toward the music that had bubbled up from the underground to take over the charts. He started the decade by covering Morrissey and by the middle of the decade, he was touring with Nine Inch Nails as his support and incorporating electronica and noisy, industrial guitars into his music. In some ways, he was just picking up on the trends of the time, but his sudden re-adoption of the concept album showed that he was also willing to move against what was popular at the time.

He was drawn back in this direction after writing music for the television drama, *The Buddha of Suburbia* (adapted from a novel by Hanif Kureishi). Usually, it wouldn't make sense to refer to a soundtrack album as being conceptual, but *The Buddha of Suburbia* (1993) only featured one song from the television

CONCEPT ALBUMS

show and the rest of the material was made up of pieces that Bowie had written around themes from the novel.

He then moved fully back into the world of concept albums with *1.Outside* (1995), which saw him collaborating with Brian Eno (somewhat ironic since it was Eno that had taken Bowie away from conceptual work in the first place). The recording was guided by a set of 'oblique strategies' which Eno created to free the musicians from their old routines. Bowie introduced randomness into his lyric writing by starting with disparate pieces of text that had been jumbled together by a computer program. During one session of recording, Bowie was hit by a burst of inspiration that saw him create the entire narrative structure in the space of three hours.

The album booklet introduced all of the new characters he created, who were all listed as coming from the fictional location of Oxford Town, New Jersey. Three pages were taken up by a biography of Nathan Adler, a detective from Art Crime Inc. He describes his investigation into the death of Baby Blue Grace, a fourteen-year-old girl whose dismembered body had been artfully arranged outside the entrance to the Oxford Town Museum of Modern Parts. Three suspects are discussed within Adler's notes: Ramona A. Stone, an artist of ill-repute; Leon Blank, whose previous crimes include 'plagiarism without a license'; and Algeria Touchshriek, who deals in 'art-drugs and DNA prints.'

The diary then skips backward and forward in time, detailing the investigation as it proceeds without giving any final clue as to its conclusion. The character, Ramona, has apparently been running a church that preaches suicide as a way to reach eternal life and she makes a living by creating jewellery made from the body parts of dead animals, though many of her customers are known to have gone missing after visiting her.

This aspect of Bowie's work was inspired by the artist, Damien Hirst, whose recent work displayed dead animals that had been cut in half and preserved in formalin.

The most striking aspect of *1.Outside* was the way it used technology to expand its storytelling scope – an early sign that the digital age might provide new possibilities for the concept album. In between the tracks on the album, the characters speak for themselves in voices that are all digital manipulations of Bowie's. The pictures supplied with the booklet have been altered and warped to give them a surreal, futuristic sheen and many also warp Bowie's image into other guises.

The use of up-to-the-minute technology did mean that some of the pieces have not survived the passing of time as well as others – the artwork looks like it's been thrown together by a teenager on Photoshop and the beats sound dated. Bowie's excitement at rediscovering his creative mojo also seems to have gotten away on him and the album is far longer (74 minutes) than the songs can justify.

Nonetheless it is remarkable that a well-established artist like Bowie was taking such risks so late in his career. This new flourishing of ideas was enough to keep his career moving

David Bowie is most lauded for his seventies concept albums, though his nineties effort – *1.Outside* – was a more complete conceptual work.
(Garry Brandon)

steadily until he was struck by a heart attack in 2004 and he then took a hiatus from music that lasted until *The Next Day* (2013). *1.Outside* didn't end up being anywhere near as influential as Bowie's early concept albums, though his return to storytelling did presage a gradual emergence of more conceptual work within the alternative rock sphere a few years later.

The desire to use digital technology to expand the world of the concept album was later taken up by The Smashing Pumpkins (whose lead singer, Billie Corgan, has repeatedly expressed his love for Bowie's music). The band had first hinted at their conceptual leanings on *Mellon Collie and the Infinite Sadness* (1995), which was a double-album with one side devoted to night and the other to day (though aside from a few songs, the concept was very loose).

Corgan hoped to construct a more complete concept on *Machina/The Machines of God* (2000) and used each of his fellow band members as the inspiration for a set of fictional characters. However his plans were ruined by the departure of bass player, D'arcy Wretzky, and this led to his plans being considerably watered down. Nonetheless, the album art featured images and writings that gave some background on the four characters that Corgan had created. More interestingly, a number of videos and websites were also made, which were going to be planted around the internet so that fans could discover the story as they went along. Sadly this project was eventually scrapped and all that remains of this aspect of the work are a few videos that have unofficially been loaded to YouTube.

To find a more complete early vision of how the internet might be used to support a concept album we have to turn to an unlikely source – the indie songwriter, John Darnielle, who releases work under the pseudonym 'The Mountain Goats.' He was hardly someone you would expect to be at the digital forefront since his early work was purposefully recorded in lo-fi, raw manner and instead gained its power from his poetic lyricism and starkly realist subject matter.

His early songs repeatedly referred to a fictional married couple that were struggling to save their fractured relationship. Fans came to know them as the 'Alpha Couple' since the songs in which they featured all had 'Alpha' in the title.

On *Tallahassee* (2002), Darnielle devoted an entire album to a crucial moment in this couple's life – they have just moved into a dilapidated house on Southward Plantation Road (in Tallahassee) and the state of their lives has become so bad that they spend most nights drinking themselves into oblivion. The album isn't as miserable as this description might suggest, since many of the songs have an upbeat energy to them (this was the first album on which Darnielle brought in a full band of musicians to accompany him).

The literary feel of the album is heightened by a written introduction that is included in the sleeve notes and, more interestingly from our current perspective, Darnielle provided a

John Darnielle of the Mountain Goats broke new ground by creating a website in support of his concept album, *Tallahasee*. *(Petra Jane Smith)*

contemporary layer to his concept album by having a website created that showed a floor plan of the house in which the alpha couple were living. Visitors to the site could click on each room to discover different items related to the story – images or small pieces of text (the site can still be found online by searching the waybackmachine.org).

Darnielle's next release, *The Sunset Tree* (2004), did have a theme of sorts – the songs were autobiographical pieces about

CONCEPT ALBUMS

his own rough childhood, but it wouldn't be until a decade later that he'd release another fully-fledged concept album, *Beat The Champ* (2015). This album is a far more musically upbeat work which follows the career of a professional wrestler. That said, it certainly doesn't shy away from the violent spectacle of a wrestling match and there is a track called 'Foreign Object' about the bringing in disallowed items into the ring to attack your opponent.

In the same year as *Tallahasee* came out, there were two other notable concept albums from within the alternative world, which also used fictional relationships as their centrepiece – *Control* (2002) by Pedro the Lion and *Amore del Tropico* (2002) Black Heart Procession. *Control* follows the decline of a young businessman who has just been fired from his job and has a failing marriage due to a regrettable extramarital affair. Pedro the Lion use this as a framework for talking about matters of love, loss and redemption from a Christian perspective, though the album's final act shows no sign of mercy – the wife discovers the affair and stabs the businessman to death. The plot of *Amore del Tropico* also follows a couple whose relationship ends in murder (in this case, while visiting Central America on holiday), though the exact storyline is a little obscure, to say the least.

As a result of all these albums, it is tempting to see 2002 as a crucial year during which the public perception of the concept album seems to change and some might also point to the album, *Yoshimi Battles the Pink Robots* (2002) by the Flaming Lips as another example. In this case, the term isn't really justified though The Flaming Lips did later move into narrative work by creating their own short film, *Christmas On Mars,* and writing all of the music for its soundtrack.

However, it is probably more correct to see the trend back towards concept albums as a more gradual change in the musical mood of the time (every trend in popular music seems to cycle back into fashion eventually). If we dig further back we can find weaker examples of concept albums that preceded this breakthrough year. One example is *The Gay Parade (*1999) by the cult band, Of Montreal, which had a song for each character in a small town who form together into a 'parade.'

Even more influential were Neutral Milk Hotel whose most admired work, *In The Aeroplace Over The Sea* (1998), was a lyrically complex work that was interwoven with a set of overlapping themes. At the heart of the album is Mangum's interest in the life of Anne Frank and her diary becomes a central thread that connects together the other material on the album – the lyrics also refer to the preserved body of a 'two-headed boy' that is similarly frozen in time for eternity, and Mangum's deep connection with these dead historical figures is presented as an extension of his own spirituality. Clearly this is a loose concept album, but it was cited as an influence by later artists who moved in a similar direction (most notably Arcade Fire, see Chapter Seven).

Taken as whole, these works show that alternative acts were becoming bored of the new minimalism that had been ushered in by grunge and the more adventurous and experimental acts were beginning to see that their work could be heightened by introducing themes and narratives that cohered across an album.

It was still a time in which the trends from underground music acts were often predictive of what would become popular in the mainstream and this was certainly the case in this instance, with a burgeoning of concept albums in the popular sphere just around the corner.

The Changing Musical Tide

The conceptual work of the hip hop and alternative rock acts covered in this chapter all show that the stigma of pretentiousness surrounding the concept album was slowly lifting by the end of the nineties. The long shadow of psychedelia and prog had now begun to fade, meaning that new artists could adopt the concept album without feeling they would be criticised for being pretentious.

The gateway to the world of concept albums had slowly been creaked open and now there would be a flood of artists willing to go through it. Their work would be less dogmatic than many of the concept albums that emerged in the seventies, but they would engage the imagination of listeners in the same manner and achieve similar levels of critical acclaim and chart-topping success.

Chapter Seven

Concept Albums in the New Millennium

Ever since they first came to prominence in the late-60s, the popularity of concept albums have been at the mercy of changes in musical fashion. At some moments, they have seemed like the perfect vehicle to enhance a musician's vision and help them reach the top of the charts, while at other times, they seemed like a fanciful indulgence that only the most experimental or underground group would undertake. The situation was particularly dire in the late eighties and early nineties, when metal musicians were the only ones who felt they could get away with taking on the form and, as a result, very few concept albums reached through to the popular consciousness.

Over the first decade of the new millennium, a new challenge emerged that would not only threaten concept albums, but the idea of an album itself. The massive expansion of the Internet made it successively easier to create digital copies of music and spread these freely on the internet. When music stores such as iTunes arrived on the scene, they made it possible for

CONCEPT ALBUMS

consumers to buy individual tracks off an album, without requiring them to be released as a stand-alone single. Some music writers began to predict that the album would soon be a thing of the past, as listeners moved towards buying only the songs they liked, rather than splashing out on a whole collection. If the album was dead, then concept albums would go along with it.

In actual fact, the trend moved in the opposite direction. Many musicians were wedded to the idea of releasing albums, often because putting out a collection of songs allowed them to express their full musical range. The idea of releasing an endless string of singles rankled them, especially since it didn't allow for more intricate, multifaceted tracks. The nature of singles is that they have to instantly grab your attention, leaving no potential for a track to be a 'slow grower.'

When asked about the death of the album by the Union Tribune in 2006, Neil Young told the interviewer: 'I know I need to make [albums] and that's all I'm concerned about. The songs are the album, and if you want to listen to one song, fine. But I try to have an album tell a story and to put them out, more than ever, in the order I wrote them.'

This was the same year that Young released his own first concept album, *Living With War* (2006), which railed against the political situation in the US. He later followed it with his paean to the electric car, *Fork In The Road* (2009), and a critique of modern agribusiness, *The Monsanto Years* (2015). Young wasn't the only artist who was inspired to make a politically charged album after the US sent its army to fight in Afghanistan and Iraq – Steve Earle opposed these wars directly on *Jerusalem* (2002) and Green Day also channelled their dissent into their work (see below). These conflicts also led to an album by English songwriter, PJ Harvey, who looked at the role of war in the history of Britain on her album, *Let England Shake* (2011).

More generally, it seemed that musicians now saw themed work as a way to place emphasis on their albums as coherent collections, which were intended to be heard together. As a result, the factors that were predicted to cause the 'death of the album' actually helped encourage a new spate of successful concept albums.

This new interest in the concept album was also aided by the breaking down of musical genres that was beginning to occur over this period. The aesthetic of the mash-up began to influence popular music and musicians now viewed the whole history of popular music as their toolkit. This led to hip hop artists using new wave synth sounds and beats that could have come from a 90s rave anthem. Meanwhile, rock increasingly made use of programmed drums, samples, turntables, and Auto-Tune. In previous decades, concept albums were seen as only being relevant within certain genres, but now there was no such concern. While the early punk groups from New York and London would've sneered at the idea of doing a concept album, the new millennium saw one of the most popular punk groups in the world releasing not one, but two of them…

Green Day

Green Day had a retro feel about their music from the start. Emerging at the tail end of the 80s in California, their singer, Billie Joe Armstrong, sang with a nasal drawl that drew straight from the English punk rockers of a decade earlier. The success of their third album, *Dookie* (1994), was the ultimate proof that punk could be repackaged as pop music (if grunge hadn't already proved the point). Yet Green Day were an amazingly long-lived musical act and they eventually grew bored with writing fast, furious punk tracks that fizzled out after a few minutes. The group decided that they wanted to expand into longer tracks that could move between different musical feels and this led to their most successful album, *American Idiot* (2004).

This shift in approach wasn't what the band had planned when they first went into the studio to record with producer, Rob Cavallo. However, the initial recording sessions were abruptly halted when the master tapes were lost (the band claimed that they'd been stolen, but later reports suggested that they may just have been erased). Cavallo suggested that they should only start the process of re-recording what they'd done if they were adamant that the songs were the best possible. Up to this point, Armstrong himself had felt uncomfortable with the sessions and felt that the expectations of his two bandmates were limiting what type of material he wrote.

After discussing these concerns in a set of band meetings, the trio returned to the studio, ready to make a fresh start. They began writing with a broader frame of reference and even started a new wave side project ('The Network'), so that they could experiment outside their usual genre. When they had enough fragments of material that they thought would suit the Green Day sound, they began knitting these brief musical ideas into longer pieces that eschewed the usual verse-chorus structure. This led to the mini-epics, 'Homecoming' and 'Jesus of Suburbia,' which Armstrong has admitted were influenced by the Who's 'A Quick One While He's Away' (which Green Day later covered during the sessions for their next album). Cavallo turned out to be the perfect producer to capture the theatrical aspirations of these new pieces since he had previously recorded soundtracks from a number of stage musicals (including the Broadway hit, *Rent*).

Armstrong's lyrics were driven by his frustration at the state of politics in the US under president, George W. Bush, and he later explained to NPR that the album was inspired by watching the invasion of Iraq live on television: 'It was like a cross between war and reality television ... [People were] so distracted by what was being shown on television ... In reality you're sitting on the couch and seeing the world explode and lives being lost before your eyes. For me, I felt this moment of rage and patriotism, if you wanna call it that, and the song "American Idiot" wrote itself in thirty seconds.'

He gradually invested his feelings into the character, St Jimmy, who is angered by the limited outlook of those around him and decides to leave the small town where he grew up and head to the city. He falls in love with a girl called 'whatsername,' but when the romance comes to an end and he's left on his own, Jimmy is left to come to terms with himself and his place in society. Armstrong told Spin magazine that the ambiguous nature of the storyline was a purposeful decision on his part: 'You have to keep your sense of humour when doing something like this, because you don't want it to sound pretentious. I like *Tommy*, but it's so literal. I didn't want to write: "Here I am, walking down the stairs, preparing some food."'

The concept was made more concrete by the extended music video for 'Jesus of Suburbia,' which showed a montage of Jimmy's life. The subsequent clip for 'Wake Me Up When September Ends' was similarly cinematic and told the story of a young man enlisting to fight in Iraq. The song itself was originally written about the death of Armstrong's father when he was child, but the mention of September surely brought to mind the 9/11 attacks in the minds of many listeners and helped add poignancy to the track. These various threads captured the imagination of the wider public and Green Day were amply rewarded with sales of the album surpassing 14 million worldwide. They also received six Grammy nominations in 2005, eventually winning 'Best Rock Album.'

Green Day's Bille Joe Armstrong playing in front of the *American Idiot* logo of a hand holding a heart-shaped grenade. *(Garry Brandon)*

21st Century Breakdown (2009), took a similar approach – Armstrong introduced two characters (Gloria and Christian) and used them as stand-ins for the positive and negative aspects of his own unrest. The overall theme was more vague on this occasion, but Armstrong told Alternative Press that he still found it useful to have a singular vision in mind: 'The songs speak to each other in the way that the songs on *Born to Run* [by Bruce Springsteen] speak to each other. I don't know if you'd call it a concept album, but there's definitely a thread that connects everything.'

Meanwhile, theatre director, Michael Mayer, had begun working with the group to turn *American Idiot* into a stage musical. The show created a more cohesive storyline from the rough sketch that had been provided by the original album, incorporating B-sides and material off *21st Century Breakdown* to fill out the production. Armstrong took the role of the main character for many of the early shows and later returned to the role when his replacement took a break to tend to personal matters. The show reached Broadway and went on to win two Tony Awards for its design and this success inspired the idea of turning it into a movie.

Green Day weren't the only band looking to build their own mythological world that their fans could tap into. The next band to try this approach was one that also brought back some of the drama of 70s shock rock...

My Chemical Romance

The lead singer of My Chemical Romance, Gerard Way, was an aspiring comic artist when he first decided to form a band and this undoubtedly fed into his decision to add narrative elements to his music. Way was profoundly affected by the September 11 attacks on New York, but he didn't incorporate it directly into his songwriting as Green Day had. Instead, Way took 9/11 as a chilling reminder of mortality and this kickstarted a new found determination to take his own ideas out into the world. One week later he formed My Chemical Romance and within a few months they were recording their first release.

I Brought You My Bullets, You Brought Me Your Love (2002) provided a vague storyline about the doomed love affair of a young couple, whose wild lifestyle leads them to be finally gunned down in the desert (as described on the track 'Demolition Lovers'). On the cover of their follow-up release, *Three Cheers For Sweet Revenge* (2004), the deceased couple is shown risen from the grave and the young woman has stitches along her neck to hold her head in place. The liner notes suggested that the couple has won their freedom from the devil, after agreeing to murder a thousand evil men on his behalf. On both these albums, the thematic elements were very thinly sketched and were only discussed by the most committed fans but Way would make a far more complete statement on their next release.

CONCEPT ALBUMS

The Black Parade (2007) revolves around a character known only as 'the patient' who is a young man looking back on his life, while he is stuck in a hospital bed dying of cancer. His imminent death has caused him to recall one of the favourite events from his life - a parade he watched as a child. Yet his illness causes him to hallucinate that the parade is a death march, which is filled with all the people who were closest to him. This parade is shown in fantastical detail on the cover of the album and also forms the centre piece of the music video for 'Welcome to the Black Parade.' The band followed the Beatles in taking on the name of a fictional band (on this occasion, a deathly marching band called 'The Black Parade') and their costumes also had a similar look, though the bold colours of psychedelia, were replaced by the black and white of emo.

Way revealed that he was partially inspired by a parade that he had seen as a child and decided it was a great symbolic image: 'there's something really cultural about a parade, which is why it became the perfect vehicle. It could represent a funeral procession, or the Day of the Dead or a celebration. For the album's character, it's what he wants death to be.'

The album as a whole has a hint of musical theatre to it and Way admitted that he was influenced by the music of composer Kurt Weill. It is therefore fitting that the band arranged a one-line cameo in 'Mama' for stage singer, Liza Minnelli, who had starred in the movie version of Kurt Weill and Bertolt Brecht's *Cabaret*. More significantly, the band brought in producer, Rob Cavallo, who had previously worked on Green Day's *American*

Idiot, suggesting that Armstrong's foray in concept albums had been an influence on Way.

Gerard found that Cavallo's production was crucial to the mood he was trying to create: 'One of the more immediate goals we discussed with Rob Cavallo was to create this world in your head. The biggest goal was to not make a record that was self-absorbed, but to make a record that was self-aware ... to really create the loudest, ultimate form of self-expression.'

During the same year, Way also found time to return to his love of comic books, by writing an impressively realised comic series, *The Umbrella Academy*. The work had originally been sketched out by Way himself, though the final version featured the stunning illustrations of Gabriel Ba. At Comic Con 2009, Way discussed his plans for a new work called *The True Lives of the Fabulous Killjoys*, which was going to be a collaboration with Shaun Simon and Becky Cloonan. The characters from this work were used as the basis of My Chemical Romance's next album, *Danger Days: The True Lives of the Fabulous Killjoys* (2010). Rather than explicating a specific story, the band instead used the characters as a source for imagery and inspiration. Each of the band members took on an alter-ego – Way was 'Party Poison,' his younger brother Mikey (the group's bassist) took the name 'Kobra Kid,' Frank Iero (the group's guitarist) became 'Fun Ghoul,' and Ray Toro (their drummer) as 'Jet Star.'

Together these characters made up a gang called 'The Killjoys' from the year 2019. The society in which they live has become repressive and dull, due to the influence of the massive corporation called Better Living Industries and the Killjoys react by heading into the desert at the outskirts of town to get into range for the rebellious radio broadcasts of DJ Death Defying. The songs on the album represented the spirit of this group rather than making specific lyrical reference to their lives and replaced the heavy orchestration of *The Black Parade*, with fast-paced poppy rock songs. Way explained that the album was intended to rely more on symbolism than storytelling: 'A lot of the elements of the setting are completely metaphorical for the real stuff that's going on in this album ... which is a struggle of art vs. commerce and filth vs. corporate clean up, and freedom being a dangerous chaotic thing that's very hard to achieve, versus a kind of utopian situation where you're very safe and everything's very easy, but it's also very boring.'

Clearly, *Danger Days*, can only be considered a very loose concept album and it is likely that *The Black Parade* will remain as the band's most thematically complete release. Their use of imagery over this period connected the band with a legion of fans who adopted the otherworldly clothing of the band. Outsiders wrote off the music and style as 'emo,' without realising that the group owed more to musical theatre than they did to the history of 'emotional hardcore' (the scene which gave 'emo' its name). In this respect, they were more similar to the artist we shall look at next than they were to other contemporary 'emo' acts, even if the actual music the artists made were worlds apart.

Janelle Monáe

The rebirth of concept albums in the new millennium wasn't only restricted to the world of rock. Janelle Monáe's album, *Archandroid* (2010) proved that funk was still a home for concept albums, even though over thirty years had passed since Parliament/Funkadelic first delved into this territory. Monáe initially gained the eye of the general public as a backing singer for Outkast and she featured in their film, *Idlewild*. This led to her being picked up by Puff Daddy's label, Bad Boy, though her vision for her music was rather different than the other artists on this label.

She began with an EP, *Metropolis, Suite I: The Chase* (2007), which introduced her alter-ego, an android named Cindi Mayweather who had illegally fallen in love with a human ('Anthony Greendown'). The pair are discovered and flee her home of Metropolis to make a new life for themselves.

Monáe had been partially inspired by the classic black-and-white film, *Metropolis*, and she made this connection even more explicit on her debut album, *Archandroid* (2010), which had a cover that showed her in a similar futuristic headdress as the android diva from the film. The booklet makes clear that the android, Cindi, was actually created from the DNA of Monáe herself and transported back from the 28th century to the 21st, so she could be reconstituted to fight against those that 'suppress freedom and love.' Her thematic approach was reminiscent of Parliament's Afro-futurism and used sci-fi imagery as a way to add a playful aspect to her songs of social critique. Her music veered between bombastic funk, backed by hip hop beats, and slower R&B numbers that also made use of the vocal chops she'd gained from studying musical theatre in her late teens. *Archandroid* was a surprise hit for Monáe and reached number seventeen on the Billboard charts. The critical reception was even stronger, with the album being nominated for a Grammy Award.

Monáe is one of only a few female artists to undertake a concept album. This may be due to the fact that many of the genres which took up the form were ones that are predominantly dominated by men (e.g., prog and heavy metal). Another unusual aspect of Monáe's work was that her interest in narrative began at the very start of her solo career. In contrast, most concept albums are attempted by established musicians who are looking for a new challenge, though the next act that we will look at also took up a conceptual approach on their first album.

Arcade Fire

Arcade Fire emerged out of the indie scene in Montreal (Canada) early in the new millennium. At the heart of the band was musical couple, Win Butler and Régine Chassagne, who decided to arrange each album around a central set of ideas and motifs. *Funeral* (2004) took its title from the fact that the band were beset by multiple deaths of family members during the period of recording the album. For Chassagne, this led to a number of mournful meditations on her family history and their connection to the struggling nation of Haiti. Butler also picked up on the funereal theme in his lyrics, though he also wrote a couple of uplifting numbers that encouraged listeners to grasp hold of life, in particular on the band's live anthem, 'Wake Up.'

Neon Bible (2007) took a similar approach of invoking a single theme, this time focusing on the power of television and its ability to reflect the outside world, without necessarily giving a true representation of it. The lyrics draw a picture of religion and politics as being twisted by this medium, leaving viewers disconnected from reality (represented on the album by the repeated metaphorical image of being lost at sea).

These efforts garnered great praise from critics and the band's fanbase continued to grow. Their use of conceptual imagery also struck a chord with David Bowie, who joined them onstage for a number of live shows and television appearances. After just two albums, they were already one of the most respected bands of their generation, though their most successful work was still ahead of them.

The Suburbs (2010) was inspired by a visit Butler took with his brother (also a member of Arcade Fire) to the neighbourhood where they both grew up in Houston, Texas. He was struck by how completely the layout of the streets had altered since their childhood and he took this as a sign of how quickly society changes in the modern era. Rather than simply dismissing suburban life in an off-hand manner, Butler told NME that his goal was 'neither a love letter to, nor an indictment of, the suburbs – it's a letter from the suburbs.'

The band made an attempt to connect their vision with the experiences of their listeners by creating an online interactive music video, which asked users to enter the 'address of the home' where they grew up and the website used Google's street view images to create a unique music video using imagery taken from around this area. The strength of the album's thematic vision also led to the filmmaker, Spike Jonze, using it as inspiration for a 30 minute short film, *Scenes From The Suburbs*.

This album completed the band's progress from indie darlings to breakthrough mainstream act, hitting the top spot on the Billboard Chart. Their previous albums had been nominated at the Grammys in the 'Best Alternative Music Album' category, but this time they made the leap to the 'Best Album' category and beat a number of higher profile acts to take the prize.

This was a final sign – if one was needed – that the concept album had been returned to its place as a viable musical form. Of course, within heavy metal this had never stopped being the case. While the breakthrough concept albums of Green Day, My Chemical Romance, Janelle Monáe, and Arcade Fire might have seemed like a new phenomenon, the continued use of the form within heavy metal was less of a surprise.

Modern Heavy Metal

One of the most bizarre concept albums to emerge out of heavy metal in the new millennium was created by a group whose music reached prog-esq levels of complexity, Mars Volta. The two core members were Omar Rodriguez-Lopez and Cedric Bixler Zavala, who'd previously played in hardcore group, At the Drive-in.

Their new approach was more progressive, but also far heavier than classic prog, though they drew a direct connection by enlisting Storm Thorgersen to design the cover of their debut album, *De-loused in the Comatorium* (2003). Thorgerson had been one of the creative forces behind the Hipgnosis design company that had done multiple Pink Floyd sleeves, as well as Genesis's *Lamb Lies Down On Broadway*. On this occasion, the image was a gold head on a plate, with a light-ray coming out of its mouth. *Deloused* was a homage to the artist and poet Julio Venegas, who'd been amongst the outsider artists that Cedric and Omar had hung around with as teenagers. According to rumour, he'd purposefully given himself a drug overdose and ended up in a coma and the album describes his dreamlike battles against the evil aspects of himself, ending with him emerging from the coma, only to commit suicide by throwing himself off a bridge onto a busy motorway. Cedric told Mojo magazine that he wasn't concerned by the dark, oblique approach of the album: 'Life isn't always pretty, it's not a three-minute pop song. As

Mars Volta's *Deloused in the Comatorium* (2003) showed all the musical complexity and lyrical obscurity of prog. It even had cover art by Storm Thorgersen. *(Storm Studios)*

surreal as the album might seem, that's how life is; you have no control over it, and sometimes it just doesn't make sense.'

Venegas had also been a smack addict and this was a burden that fell across the members of Mars Volta themselves, so the album can also be interpreted as a metaphor for the band's struggle to free themselves. Sadly, the group's bass player, Jeremy Ward, died of a drug overdose a month before the album came out and it was this final tragedy that led Omar and Cedric to finally quit heroin themselves.

Emerging out of Atlanta, Mastodon brought a more sludgy sound to metal music, while retaining a high level of musicianship and extravagant lyrical content. The band broke through to a wider audience with their second album, *Leviathan* (2004), which was based on the classic novel *Moby Dick* by Herman Melville. The music was by turns grand and vicious, managing to encapsulate the extreme ups and downs of hunting a giant whale and putting one's life at risk to bring it home. Guitarist, Bill Kelliher, told the Guardian that they found their own way to relate to the original tale: '*Leviathan* was about chasing the whale, the sacrifice we made every day. We had a big white van, which we all piled into and kissed our families goodbye, just like the sailors going off to chase that whale.'

The inspiration for their next album, *Blood Mountain* (2006), was less specific, though there was clearly a quest narrative at the heart of the storyline. The hero of the piece is climbing the mountain to retrieve a crystal skull which will allow him to reach the next stage of evolution, but his path brings him into battle with a number of ferocious creatures. The growing power of the group's music saw them nominated for a Grammy Award for 'Best Metal Performance' for the song, 'Colony of Birchmen' from this album.

The band abandoned the conceptual approach on *Crack The Skye* (2009), though it is interesting to note that the group's first four albums take the same overall pattern as the early King

Crimson albums – each relating to one of the basic elements of Water, Earth, Air, and Fire (the latter was a loose theme on Mastodon's debut album, *Remission*, 2002).

Mastodon are hardly alone in keeping the concept album alive in metal, especially amongst acts with a prog tendency to their music, such as: Alesana, Dominici, and Ayurveda. One of the most striking of these new prog-influenced acts are Coheed and Cambria, who have used a sci-fi tale written by their lead singer, Claudio Sanchez, to inspire many of the songs throughout their fifteen year career. The tale has also spawned a novel and set of comics under the title, *The Amory Wars*. These albums are an ongoing testament to the association between heavy metal and the concept album, and this trend shows no sign of fading away any time soon.

Hip hop

Hip hop's early interest in album-length storytelling soon faded after the disappearance of pioneering acts like Prince Paul, Deltron 3030, and The Streets. Part of the reason for this may have been that hip hop had truly pushed itself to the centre of popular music and even many of the most commercial pop hits made liberal use of hip hop sounds or introduced a verse of rapping before the final chorus (in the place where a guitar solo would've formerly been).

Nonetheless, the conceptual strain in British hip hop started by The Streets was eventually brought back to life by the release

of *The Defamation of Strickland Banks* (2010) by Plan B (the p
of rapper, Ben Drew). The rough storyline followed the wrongful imprisonment of a soul singer called Strickland Banks and his struggles to survive prison and be set free. This release reached the top of the UK charts and gave Drew the idea of creating a film version by patching together the relating music videos with some newly shot additions (though completion was interrupted by the release of Drew's feature-length crime film, *Ill Manors* in 2011).

Deltron 3030 also returned after a decade of silence with *Event 2* (2013), which updated their dystopian view of the future (even if the music wasn't much of an update from their former sound). The album opens with a scene-setting introduction by actor Joseph Gordon-Levitt and the star appearances continue throughout the album with the voices of comedian David Cross singer Zack De La Rocha (Rage Against the Machine), rappers The Lonely Island, and – most unexpectedly - celebrity chef David Chang.

Yet the most complete hip hop concept album of recent times was *Twelve Reasons to die* (2013) by Ghostface Killah (from the Wu-Tang Clan). The project began when Bob Perry from Soul Temple Records approached producer Adrian Younge about collaborating with the Wu-Tang Clan. The pair ended up formulating a rough story for a hip hop album with Ghostface Killah in mind, since his rap style was seen to suit the bombastic story that had sketched out. The plot was written around Ghostface Killer's alternative rapper name, Tony Starks, and the character is a mob killer for the De Luca crime family in Italy. He makes the risky move of deciding to go into business for himself and ends up being by betrayed by his girlfriend, who leads him into the hands of the De Lucas. They decide to make an example of him by executing him in a gruesome manner – dropping him into a vat of hot vinyl. Twelve records are pressed from this vinyl and given to heads of the gang, but Starks' ghost re-emerges each time the songs are played, allowing him to exact revenge on his murderers.

A sequel set in New York was released a few years later – *Twelve Reasons to Die Part II* (2015) – and this also featured another Wu-Tang Clan member, Raekwon, as a black gangster fighting another wing of the De Lucas family. He learns of the existence of Tony Starks and a new chapter of the story begins.

On both albums, Adrian Younge takes equal parts inspiration from Ennio Morricone and RZA to ensure Ghostface's story reaches cinematic heights of drama. The result is a pair of releases that prove that the legacy of hip hop concept albums is in safe hands.

Concept Albums into the Future

The examples given above are just the most obvious examples of a trend that continues to build up steam. The challenge of digital downloading is only one influence on this uptake of the concept album and many artists are beginning to see that producing conceptual work also allows them to take advantage of the positive aspects of digital technology. If they ha central theme then this can be extended across their album artwork, music videos, and websites to give a sense of grandeur to each new release.

While the examples given above are largely American, we can see that the influence of the concept album is also present in releases from the other side of the Atlantic as well. Welsh pop act, Marina and the Diamonds, themed her debut album, *Electra Heart* (2011), around the stereotypes of the modern American women. Aside from singing about these emblematic characters, she also used them as inspiration for her music videos and posted photographs of herself dressed in each style on her website and asked her fans to contribute their own images.

Around the same time, one of England's most popular acts, Coldplay, also used a conceptual approach to provide a wider basis for their album, *Mylo Xyloto* (2011). Underlying the songs is a futuristic love story written by lead singer, Chris Martin, and comic artist, Mark Osborne. It follows 'Mylo' as he searches out an underground community of 'sparkers' who cover the city in fluorescent graffiti, in defiance of a ban imposed by 'Major Minus' and the totalitarian government that he represents. Mylo falls in love with one of the sparkers, Xyloto, and the pair make plans to escape the city. The lyrics only made vague references to this tale, but it was given life in the music video for 'Hurts Like Heaven' (directed by Osborne) and he also used it as the plot of a comic book series. *Mylo Xyloto* provides another example of the fact that artists no longer have to rely on putting out all the information about their conceptual ideas within the album itself, since they can use their artwork, website content, and music videos to expand on the world they have created.

It might be remarked that the narrative concept albums covered in this chapter are mostly quite weak versions of the form – with only patchy storylines to hold them together. Nonetheless, the wide variety of artists who have tried to introduce themes or storytelling into their albums shows that the influence of the concept album is stronger than ever. And have we've seen in the earlier chapters, even some of the most well-known concept albums were often thin on connecting tissue when examined more closely.

In fact, it appears as if the conceptual approach has reached a new level of popularity that matches its first rise in the psychedelic and prog eras. Digital technology may have initially been seen as a challenge to the idea of collecting songs together for simultaneous release as an 'album,' but in the end it wasn't enough to threaten this linchpin of popular music tradition. Instead, the possibilities offered by new technology have put more power in the hands of artists and made it easier for them to advance over-arching themes in their work. Even newer musical acts don't need to seek permission from their record labels to pursue conceptual projects since the cost of digital recording is much cheaper, which may explain why acts like Janelle Monáe and Arcade Fire were able to move in this direction from the very start of their careers.

CONCEPT ALBUMS IN THE NEW MILLENIUM

The goal of a concept album remains the same as it has always been – to take the listening experience beyond the range of a set of individual songs and engage the listener's own imagination to create a broader, more expansive sense of what the music is trying to evoke. It is this goal that will keep musicians returning to the form over the decades to come and ensure that concept albums have a role to play in music into the future.

CPSIA information can be obtained
at www.ICGtesting.com
Printed in the USA
LVOW04s1519220916
505789LV00049B/548/P